THE FIVE SCHOOLS OF BORDER CONTROL

1. I'M OK, YOU'RE OK SCHOOL

MEMBERS: Irish setters, retrievers, pointers, Weimaraners, otterhounds . . .
POLICY: When a thief, kidnapper or homicidal maniac happens by the property, assume he's a friend of the family and let him into the house as long as he passes the secret test: he throws the ball for you first.

2. WALL OF SOUND SCHOOL

MEMBERS: Chihuahuas, schnauzers, cockers, toy poodles, dachshunds . . .
POLICY: If anybody approaches the border, start barking like crazy and don't stop no matter what. If they keep coming, either head for cover and hit new decibels—or charge their shoes, fall back and repeat.

3. MAKE MY DAY SCHOOL

MEMBERS: German shepherds, Dobermans, pit bulls, Rottweilers, anything with an important bone, fed up or in heat.
POLICY: If a visitor happens by without your owner as a personal chaperon, assume that they are a blood donor.

4. ENIGMATIC SCHOOL

MEMBERS: Newfoundlands, borzois, Great Danes, malamutes, huskies, anything part wolf, or schizoid mutts.
POLICY: When anybody steps past your fence line, track their progress with your pupils, not your entire head. When they come within range, reach out their hand and say, "Hey, poochie, do you bite?", answer either by amputating or by ignoring them—depending on your mood.

5. THE YELLOW SCHOOL

MEMBERS: Anything chicken, shy or just fixed.
POLICY: No matter what you see—hide.

FOR
DOGS
ONLY!

DAVID COMFORT

How to Live with
Human Beings

For Mom & Dad,
   This must be read
aloud every day to your
dog - so he will know
exactly how to behave
around humans.
      Purchased during our
honeymoon to Banner Elk, April,
                                    1990.

POCKET BOOKS

New York   London   Toronto   Sydney   Tokyo

Bruce & Brenda

To my devoted collaborators

An *Original* Publication of POCKET BOOKS

POCKET BOOKS, a division of Simon & Schuster Inc.
1230 Avenue of the Americas, New York, NY 10020

ISBN: 0-671-66764-5

First Pocket Books trade paperback printing February 1989

10   9   8   7   6   5   4   3   2   1

POCKET and colophon are trademarks of
Simon & Schuster Inc.

Printed in the U.S.A.

CONTENTS

INTRODUCTION

To Human Beings

About five billion human beings live on earth right now. We are the most widespread mammal on the planet. For a simple reason: we run it.

The second most populous animal on earth is our best friend: the dog. To every twenty human beings there is about one dog. About 250 million dogs inhabit the world at present.

But in spite of this population, to say nothing of need, never in history has a book been written for dogs.

Why?

First, dogs can't read. This text will lay claim to many abilities canines have that human beings don't yet know about. One of them is not that they are literate. So it will be necessary, though at this point it may seem unlikely, for human beings to read this book out loud to their dogs.

But again—why?

What is in this work that will interest the average dog?

As the title suggests, this book tells him or her how to live with human beings. In this respect, it is a survival guide. Of course, generally, dogs get along very well with people. Their unique ability to do so has allowed them to prosper over the years. But it has taken compromise on their part. Great compromise. Most objective owners will admit that their dog has come more than halfway in their relationship. And if the human being can admit this, how much more prevalent must this opinion be among his "best friends"?

This book intends to lighten the weight of that compromise and increase the harmony between canines and humans. In a world that is otherwise disharmonious, why not concentrate on what is good and work to make it better?

Whether it is a Saint Bernard or terrier, a Doberman or chow, young or old, a car chaser or a coucher, in the following pages your dog will be taken through every dimension of life—from puppyhood to old age. And, with the help of visual aids, your dog will be given a new view on everything so that the joys of his life with people will be increased.

From the beginning of time dogs have served human beings with a fidelity that has gone beyond the survival instinct. This in spite of the fact that people, having spent the better part of their history in civil war, cannot seem to live with themselves. True, dogs fight sometimes, too. But they have not invented the bomb. Still, they love us.

So dogs are saintly. (As we know, *dog* is *god* spelled backward.) As is commonly acknowledged, life as a saint is not easy. It is full of great compromise and service to people, often without thanks. Yet dogs continue their saintly tasks.

Even so, many of you are skeptical about the idea of reading this book to dogs. Think of it as an acknowledgment of all they mean to us, and an effort to come halfway for the first time and try to make their life with us easier.

When the idea of talking to plants and playing music for them first came out, people had mixed reactions. But the plants of those who tried it began suddenly to thrive like never before. Other plants just kept dying like they always had.

And how much smarter are dogs than plants?

The next question is: What are the author's credentials? What qualifies him to write a book on this subject, to this audience?

But this is not something dogs care about. Having themselves never attended a university, our friends don't expect or have a high opinion of degrees or titles. What they do have regard for, though, are the studies in which we are all undergraduates: call it the School of Life, and of Instinct. Studies which give no letters behind someone's name, but something far more convincing. At least to dogs.

Beyond that, the author will not make any unbelievable claims for himself: such as that he is half dog or his distant ancestors were dogs or even that he was suckled by dogs. No. For better or worse the author is a full human being. But he was born and brought up with dogs; in the course of life has spent many hours studying them, talking with them, and learning their secrets; and has received many recent requests from them—in spite of his unworthiness—to take up his pen now and share the fruits of that collaboration. For the improvement of nature's finest friendship.

Now, the last question is: Does your dog really need this book? To determine the answer, take the following quiz.

INTRODUCTORY QUIZ:
WHETHER YOUR DOG NEEDS THIS BOOK

---

1. Is your dog moody, off his food, wagging his tail less, or subject to unexplainable nightmares? YES NO
2. Have you ever caught your dog staring at you? Then either: a. Quickly looking away? b. Trying to pretend he hasn't been staring? c. Sharpening his stare? (Any or all) YES NO
3. Has your dog ever suddenly, for no apparent reason, sighed? YES NO
4. Does your dog ever give you less than the greeting you expect or would like when you get up in the morning, come home from work, return from vacation? YES NO

---

5. When you enter a room your dog is already in, does he ever: a. Lower his ears? b. Ignore you? c. Leave the room? (Any or all)   YES NO

6. (Try to be especially honest here): Have you ever scolded your dog for doing something you would have had a hard time not doing yourself had you been in his paws, or for not doing something you would have had a hard time doing yourself?   YES NO

7. Does your dog ever: a. Not come when he is called? b. Jump into strangers' cars? c. When you have house guests, sleep with them instead of you? (Any or all)   YES NO

8. Has your dog ever attacked you?   YES NO

9. Have you ever been told by someone (human), especially a friend or member of your family, you are hard to get along with, at least occasionally?   YES NO

10. Are you perfect?   YES NO

If your answer to any of Introductory Quiz questions 1 through 9 is a Yes, your dog needs this book.

If your answer to question 10 is No, your dog needs this book.

Now, if you love your dog, you will read him this book. If you don't, you won't.

All right. You have decided to read your dog the book. In short, we are ready to begin. What do you do now?

First, call your dog in. If he is an outside dog, let him indoors anyway. Please. Just this once. He'll know it is for a special occasion. If he is an inside dog already but isn't allowed on the furniture, invite him up on the couch with you anyway. Just this once. If he is used to all these privileges, just turn off the TV and put on your glasses.

Now be forewarned. When you begin to read, do not expect any signs of humanlike attentiveness from your dog. Do not throw down the book impatiently if you cannot see any. Do not feel like a fool. If your dog's concentration seems to immediately stray, his mind elsewhere, eyes moving from distraction to distraction in the room, don't bother yourself. It's natural. Keep reading. Your dog is just getting used to the novelty of being read to, addressed like the sensitive, intelligent creature he is, of having his hidden thoughts spoken for the first time in his life, and of hearing solutions to his greatest problems getting along with you.

All these things will make him edgy, distractible. He may even go to the kitchen or utility room for a drink of water. Don't stop him. He'll get dry during this book. Keep reading, slightly louder; or wait till he comes back.

Third, it may happen that he will fall asleep immediately—as if your reading bores or sedates him. Nothing could be further from the truth. What human beings take for sleep in a dog is usually a deep, highly receptive alpha state. Your dog may very well enter it after only a few sentences in order to better take this book in.

So, again—*keep reading*. These reactions from your dog are only natural. This is the first book that has ever been written for him—in history.

Last, do not interrupt to explain a certain word or concept to your friend. There is no word and no concept in this text that your dog is not familiar with, even if long ago you decided he is not bright.

If people learn nothing else from this book, I hope it will be that dogs can no longer be judged in human terms. And that what seems to be the case with them as often as not isn't the case.

On that note, we are ready.

There is only one thing left to be done.

Insert your finger behind this page, at Chapter 1. Look up. Glance at your dog next to you, ready on the couch now, ears cocked. Smile at him. And say this:

"I'm probably completely crazy, but there is something I'd like to read to you. It is a book about how to get along with us human beings better, and I'm reading it to you because I love you and know it's not always easy."

GETTING
ADOPTED

INTRODUCTION

The Difference Between Dogs and Human Beings

Dogs—whether you are young, old, or middle-aged now—none of you will forget the first major problem you faced.

Getting Adopted. By a human being.

Most other animals are lucky enough to stay with their parents, or at least their mom, until they are almost grown up and ready to go out on their own. But not you dogs, or at least not most of you.

One of your first memories is probably of a human being. The sound of a voice; the sensation of ten fingers cuddling you; or the

sight, when your eyes opened after a week, of one human or a group standing tall as Empire State Buildings around your whelping box, wearing clothes, wide smiles, and chattering in a strange tongue.

All you could see was how different we are from you. People, too, are impressed by these differences, on all levels—physical, social, and mental. Here they are now from our point of view. (see page 11)

The question, then, is: with such differences, why did people start adopting you dogs? Indeed, how did our species even get together in the first place?

Scientists say the fact that we both eat meat and love company was the original rationale, 360 thousand years ago, when we were still apes and you were wolves. It was a hunting partnership. We were the brains of the team; you provided your 195 million more olfactory cells, four legs, and your ability to do the hundred, five seconds faster than Carl Lewis. Even though we just had two legs, needed fire to stay warm, and sticks and stones to fight, something about our ridiculousness attracted you. There must be a catch, you thought. Rightly. Because now, a few ages later, we have the bomb, the space shuttle, and museums where we display the skeletons of those who used to say we would never make it.

Between the old days and now, you dogs have been at our side continually. In 3000 B.C. you greyhounds raced for pharaoh, you spitzes fought in Babylon, and you chows protected China. Two millennia hence, the Phoenicians exported you Tibetan mastiffs to Europe, you Pekingese to Crete, and you Maltese everywhere. In 75 A.D. your first famous actor and magician, Zippico the poodle, immortalized in Plutarch, enchanted the Roman emporer Vespasian. In another millennium, Genghis Khan and his grandson Kublai were hunting with five thousand hounds. Three centuries later Queen Elizabeth sicked eight hundred of you mastiffs on the Irish. Across the world fifty Chinese Imperial Ch'ins were popping out of courtiers' kimono sleeves and standing at attention on their hind legs every time the empress entered the throne room. Soon Louis XV and Madame Pompadour amused themselves on lazy

THE HUMAN-DOG DIFFERENCE CHART

HUMAN	DOG
Physical	
1. We have two legs, a thumb, and walk upright.	1. You have four legs, a dew claw, and walk horizontally.
2. We are divided into whites, blacks, reds, and yellows.	2. You are divided into the sporting group, working group, hounds, terriers, toys, and non-sporting group.
3. We wash, brush our teeth, and use toilet paper.	3. You lick yourself.
4. We trust our eyes.	4. You trust your nose.
5. We use the toilet.	5. You drink out of the toilet.
6. Carl Lewis does the 100 in 9 seconds.	6. An old greyhound does it in 4.
7. Our life expectancy is 72 years, and we say, "Heaven help us."	7. Your life expectancy is 12 years, and you say, "What the hell."
SOCIAL	
1. We shake hands.	1. You smell you-know-whats.
2. We work 9 to 5 and hate it.	2. You sleep and play around the clock and love it.
3. We bomb countries and still look over our shoulder.	3. You bite a mailman and hack around with your ball afterward.
4. We have guilty sex with select partners.	4. You have great sex with anybody, including your mother.
5. We buy property.	5. You piss on it.
MENTAL	
1. We talk (4,000 languages, 40,000 dialects, 100,000 words each).	1. You bark (7 ways, see Chapter IV, "Annoying Habits").
2. We believe in God.	2. You believe in Alpo.
3. Our accomplishments: Theory of Relativity, Model T, *Hamlet*, Beethoven's Ninth, Ceiling of Sistene Chapel, *Guernica*.	3. Your accomplishments: Your last pile in the back yard.
4. Our Favorite Films: (Serious) *Gone with the Wind* (Light) *Snow White and the Seven Dwarfs*.	4. Your favorite films: (Serious) *Lassie Come Home* (Light) *101 Dalmations*.
5. Our Heroes: Jesus, Shakespeare, Michael Jackson.	5. Your heroes: Rin Tin Tin, Lassie, Benji.

afternoons before the Revolution by watching the Chien Gris hounds of the court ferret truffles under the beeches of La Muette Park. Finally, in 1859, in Newcastle, England, fifty of you setters and pointers participated in the first dog show.

Now, in 1988, after 360 thousand years of partnership, though dog and human differences are undiminished, some say that we have become one underneath. That inside every modern person is a dog, and vice versa. Anyway, we have become an unbreakable pair. And in 1988 people don't adopt you so much for battle, the hunt, or to find us truffles, but for the simple pleasure of sharing modern life and the sofa with you.

I. Adoption Problems for Puppies

So, dogs, the first problem you all face as puppies is finding the right human to live with. You are put in this predicament as much to your surprise as anyone else's, in one of four ways.

A. FOUR PUPPY PREDICAMENTS

1. THE NEWSPAPER
You are six or eight weeks old and, without warning, find yourself and your brothers and sisters advertised in what you were born on and have been relieving yourself on: the local newspaper. In your ad are strange words such as *AKC registered, shots, marvelous with children, adorable;* and at the end is a price, a barter item, or the word *FREE.*

2. THE PET STORE
You and your brothers and sisters are out in the utility room in a cardboard box nursing your mom peacefully when all at once the man of the house bursts in followed by his wife. A few minutes

later, they throw the box into the station wagon and take you for a dizzying ride, you find yourself in the window of a bright, linoleum-tiled room filled with cages containing hamsters, rabbits, kittens, snakes, fish, and birds. Your mom is gone, you and your brothers and sisters are clawing the walls, crying, and it feels like the end of the world.

3. THE FLEA MARKET
Instead, the station wagon stops at a huge market or mall the next Saturday morning. Your mom's owner sits down next to your box all day there and gives imploring looks to passersby.

4. THE POUND
The last way it happens is the hardest of all. Your mom is temporarily between situations herself and has you under somebody's back porch or in their crawlspace. You and the rest of the litter are huddled around her one afternoon when she suddenly lets out a low growl as the beam of a flashlight hits you. On the other end of it you see a guy in uniform holding a long pole, his mouth open.

"Holy Moley, Jack—no wonder these people were complaining. This girl's got a whole day care center under here. Better get the muzzle. . . . Come on, sweetheart, let's come out here, now, nobody's going to hurt your babies. We're just taking a little ride."

An hour later you are at the pound, your mom is in the next room being checked for rabies, and the Animal Control officer is in Emergency waiting for the results.

B. FATE, BREED, AND SALESMANSHIP

No matter how you got into the Predicament, it amounted to the same thing: you were up for Adoption.

Adoption, as all you dogs know, is a crapshoot. There is no way to predict who, out of five billion human beings, will answer your ad in the paper, or happen by the pet store or pound after your arrival there yourself.

In short, the first ingredient of your Adoption is FATE. Which, unfortunately, you can't do anything about.

The second ingredient is BREED. Which you can't do anything about, either.

Even so, your Breed tells human adopters two important things. First, it tells us how you will *look* when you grow up. Since a person starts resembling his dog within a year or so, it's important that your snapshots in canine encyclopedias don't repulse him. Second, breed also tells us what kind of *personality* you might have: whether you will ride in strangers' cars and play ball with burglars breaking into our house—retrievers; or whether you will hide You-Know-What behind the furniture, bark in twenty-four-hour shifts, and relandscape the yard for one renegade mole— Lhasa apsos; or whether we will have to up our homeowner's liability coverage for mailmen, real estate agents, and Jehovah's Witnesses—pit bulls, shepherds, Dobermans, Rottweilers, mastiffs, Akitas, dachshunds.

The other important thing to us about Breed is whether you are a pedigree or a mutt. As much as people support the idea of equality and intermarriage otherwise, we have a thing about class and purity when it comes to pets. A person can sell a purebred; he's lucky if he can give away a mutt.

But, mutts, don't give up hope. You can turn the tables in your favor through the third and most important factor in Adoption: SALESMANSHIP.

Good Salesmanship is based on showing off the most irresistible qualities of your product to the consumer. For puppies— mixed or pure, no matter your Breed—your strong point is *Cuteness*. Nothing in the world is cuter to a human than a puppy, any puppy. Even you pugs, Shar-peis, Chinese cresteds, bull terriers, Pekingese, griffons, and Mexican hairless.

Cuteness is a combination of irresistible looks, priceless mannerisms, playfulness, cuddliness, and a disarming, indiscriminate love for everybody.

When one of you puppies—even without papers—turns on the Cuteness, the average human being will fall to his knees.

That's Sales.

II. The Encyclopedia of Dog Shoppers

But before you turn on the Salesmanship, first decide what kind of people are best for you to go home with. You want the very finest humans available, just like they want the finest dog available. So, to help you choose, here is the Encyclopedia of Dog Shoppers.

COUPLE WITH KIDS

1. *Couple A with Kids*
Either the husband, wife, or both, don't really like dogs. They are just getting you as a toy for their kids. Soon their kids will grow tired of you, and the parents will get stuck feeding and walking you. This annoys them. Also, you may be ruining the lawn, knocking the kids down, eating shoes, staining the carpets, et cetera. (For details, see Chapter IV, Bad Habits). So, finally, here's what usually happens before you even grow up: you get dumped. In short, you're probably talking a temporary situation and/or not getting treated right with Couple A.

2. *Couple B with Kids*
They love you dogs independently of their kids, and as more than toys. You become a brother or a sister in the family. They fill albums with more photos of you than anybody else. Later you go to college with the kids. When you die the family enshrines you in the backyard.

Ideal Couple-With-Kids Dogs
Any of you who don't mind being ridden, having your tail pulled, or being tortured with peanut butter sandwiches and Oreos. Retrievers, setters, spaniels, hounds.

COUPLE WITHOUT KIDS

1. *Couples that Had Kids Years Ago*
2. *Couples that Haven't Had Any Kids*
   a. *They Can't Have Any*
   b. *They Don't Want Any*

In all cases, the couple is usually shopping for a kid surrogate. This is an ideal situation for a dog. It means permanency and good love. Though that love may take the form of a prison occasionally—like during mating season when you want to take French Leave—this is a small price to pay for yummies, car, bed, and sofa privileges. The only time it may backfire on you is in the case of Couple 2b. Your adoption could inspire them to have a real kid, causing them, after its birth, to start ignoring you.

Ideal Couple-Without-Kids Dogs
Any of you who do mind being ridden, having your tail pulled, or being tortured with peanut butter sandwiches and Oreos. Pit bulls, Dobermans, Lhasas, spitzes, Chihuahuas.

SINGLE GUYS

1. *Young Single Guys* (Students, playboys, or looking to settle down)·
   The Young Single Guy will roughhouse with you, play Frisbee with you, take you jogging. You will be his best buddy. You might get beer instead of biscuits. He'll let you sleep on his bed because it's on the floor and he never changes the sheets anyway. But you may spend a lot of time solo in his rec room, his car, or on a chain while he dates women. Since the first priority of the average Young Single Guy is women—or, to be more specific, sex—be prepared to play second fiddle to it from Day One. So, he may at any time, without consulting you, get seriously involved and/or married and/or get her in trouble (having a kid, and we have already discussed the ramifications of that).

Ideal Young-Single-Guy Dogs
Those of you looking for an active, carefree lifestyle. Labs, dalmatians, weimaraners, German shorthaireds, Saint Bernards, sheepdogs.

2. *Middle-aged Single Guys* (Bachelors, divorced, widowed, guys pursuing alternative lifestyles)
Here you can be in for almost anybody. The chanciest is probably the guy whose marriage is on the rocks, and shows signs of being on the rebound when he enters the pet store—unironed clothes, erratic behavior, mumbling non sequiturs about his former wife while sorting through your litter. Avoid getting Cute or overly forward with him if, in response to a question from the pet store owner like "Are you looking for a dog, or a bitch, sir?" he flies off the handle.

Ideal Middle-aged-Single-Guy Dogs
Those of you ready for a more subdued and possibly complicated lifestyle. Airedales, Afghans, terriers, bulldogs, borzois, poodles, bassets, boxers, chows.

3. *Old Single Guys*
Old Single Guys are your best bet security-wise. Expect a quieter, more even-keeled life. Long slow walks. Being reminisced to about his former career or deceased wife. Watching bowl games or PGA action on weekends. And scoring his doggy bag from the Swedish smorgy on Sunday evenings.

The only possible drawback with older guys, women, too, is that you must not have any objection to getting fixed or spayed. In the case of you bitches, elderly people don't appreciate having their condo turned into Troy twice a year. As for you guy dogs, they don't like you pacing and whining all spring and fall just because they won't let you out to swarm Helen's condo. Younger humans tend to be more tolerant of sex sieges.

Ideal Old-Single-Guy Dogs
Same as Middle-aged-Single-Guy Dogs—those of you who can forget about sex.

SINGLE WOMEN

1. *Young Single Women*
2. *Middle-aged Single Women*
3. *Old Single Women*

Women, all of them, 1 through 3, tend to be more patient and understanding than men. Especially with you dogs. For instance, on lead when you are looking for The Spot To Go, not just *a spot;* or when you have an accident in the house; or when you accidentally tear up the sofa. Women won't take out their moods on you as much, physically. Also, in the case of widows, and even some divorcées, many, scorning smorgy or TV dinner leftovers, will actually cook for you.

So, if it is a toss-up between a guy and a woman for your adoption, choose the woman. Especially if you are a bitch.

Ideal Single-Woman Dogs
You fall into the same groups here as with Single Men. Except, if you are especially little, finicky, or high-strung—Pekingese, pugs, Shih Tzus, Japanese spaniels, griffons, Australian silkies, etc. —find yourself a nice older woman.

II

BOOT CAMP

INTRODUCTION

Names, Tags, and Licensing

Dogs, the first thing you get from a human being is your NAME.

It may be something one of the kids thought up on the way home from the pet store in the station wagon (Jingles, Pickles, Lollipop). Or, if your new owner is a Young Single, it could be the same as an NFL, movie, or rock 'n' roll star's (Bono or Sting). Or, if you have been Adopted by a Couple Without Kids, maybe it's the name intended for their first child (Vicki, Elizabeth, Felix). Or, if you get adopted by a Middle-aged Divorced Guy, perhaps he will name you after his lawyer, accountant, or psychiatrist (Ron, Stanley, Dr. Kauffman). A widow may ordain you in memory of the maître d' or waitress at the chateau where she and her husband honeymooned long ago (thus, Pepe, Michelle, Tasia).

Whatever the name, and whether or not you identify with it, it will affect you. There is no way you will turn out the same if you are called Boomer or Puccini, Zsa Zsa or Juice.

Unless you run away, go underground, and surface in another

neighborhood incognito or with an alias, you will hear the name many times in the next ten to fifteen years.

After deciding on your name, your new people may write it on a Milk Bone box top along with their address and phone number. Soon it comes back on a metal tag, which they put on your collar.

At the same time you get two other tags to carry.

1. **Dog License:** This is an annual fee for living. After your people pay it, you are allowed to live wherever you do for a year without getting kidnapped by other humans and driven to the pound.
2. **Rabies Tag:** Rabies is a disease that makes you go berserk and attack human beings indiscriminately, sending them to the hospital, where they receive a battery of shots in the stomach. So, we vaccinate you against this as a puppy, and issue you another tag.

You have now been initiated into the human world. You have your Name, Tags, and Shots. You're a soldier. A recruit. And ready for Boot Camp.

I. Housebreaking

A. HOW HUMAN BEINGS FEEL ABOUT YOU-KNOW-WHAT

As soon as you trot through the door of your new home (in case of roadblocks here, see Chapter V, Privileges, "The Invasion"), people will spread newspapers on the floor, although you haven't the slightest idea why. Not that you are a stranger to the tabloid. You were probably born on one. When you opened your eyes a week later, the first thing you saw was the President of the United States at a podium, a quarterback being sacked, the Dow Jones graph, a local murderer, or a jackhammered truck on a local interchange.

So, deciding not to worry about it, you trot off the Business section and begin exploring your new home under the watchful eye of your new people.

You are not at it long before, without thinking—why should you?—you pause for relief. Suddenly you hear:

"No, Boomer (Zsa Zsa, Pudgy Boy, Smoky, whatever your name is)—bad dog!"

Then they give you a spank and hurry you, howling and crying, back onto the President or outside.

In the next weeks this scene repeats itself. A few times for you German shepherds and boxers. Thousands for you bassets and Lhasa apsos. Until finally it occurs to most of you (except bassets and Lhasas) that people have an irrational feeling about You-Know-What indoors.

They don't like it.

You infer this from your three new human words: *No, bad* and *dog*. With your name, your vocabulary now stands at four words.

As for "You-Know-What," we needn't define it here because You Know What it is. As you also know, it comes in two kinds: #1 and #2. Your people use a sponge and Brawnies on the former. A pooper scooper, zip locks, a sponge, Brawnies, Lysol, and vinegar on the latter. Just from the equipment list, you see why #2 pisses us off more.

There's only one thing you don't understand. When a person goes to the bathroom in the house, how come you never see anyone grabbing their collar, throwing them onto newspaper or outdoors, yelling, "No, *bad* dog!"

An even more confusing situation is getting Housebroken with a cat around. For example, your people have just nailed you again for some You-Know-What they have found behind the living room couch, you are cowering in the pantry, tail between your legs, when the cat strolls in (you know how they stroll), cracks a Mona Lisa smile (you also know the kind), and says:

"Check this one out, dog."

He saunters into his personal lav. Here your people don't let him just relieve himself. That wouldn't be enough. Oh, no. They let him *stockpile* and *play with* his You-Know-What in a sandbox. As a result, vapors escape from under the door daily, hourly, which make the entire house smell like a guano factory. A moment later, when the cat emerges from his facilities, the fumes enough to down buffalo, a singsong voice comes from the living room—"Here, kitty. Oh, good kitty kitty!" He winks at you and snickers:

"Nothing like a good one in the house."

The first hurdle in getting Housebroken, then, isn't learning that You-Know-What belongs outside. But why the law only applies to yours. You refuse to accept that your Y-K-W is more disgusting than a cat's—on principle! Finally, there is the sentimental issue: the feeling among you that your Y-K-W on the carpet makes for a homier atmosphere.

B. THE IMPORTANCE OF MORAL SUPPORT

Since Housebreaking can be a bewildering and emotionally draining experience, not just for the human being, having Moral Support is important. If at all possible, try to get broken with somebody else, ideally a brother or sister. Almost any puppy, however, will do. Together, you don't feel singled out; you can probably crack the Housebreaking mystery faster, and when there is only one pile on the floor, you can sometimes get out of it because the human doesn't know whose it is. (But by the same token you may take stripes for work that isn't yours.)

If you can't get broken with somebody else, and have to go solo, at least keep your paws crossed for an older dog in the house who will show you the ropes. If, however, he is a Doberman, pit, spitz, or basset, he may feel that since he didn't get any shortcuts through hell, why should he give you a break? But if you play

your cards right and he is a golden retriever or sheepdog, he might come around. Especially if there are cats in the house and your mentor has been waiting for reinforcements.

C. HOW TO HIDE YOU-KNOW-WHAT

Hiding You-Know-What is an elusive art. Just about everybody has tried it at least once (not just you dogs) and struck out. The alarming failure rate has as much to do with the difficulty of camouflaging Y-K-W as the number of people on the lookout for your brand in the living room. Also, being essentially a weasely thing to do, hiding You-Know-What is not a dog's forte. But sometimes humans leave you with no choice. Where should you strike?

Right Out in Plain Sight. This is often the best hiding place for other objects because it's where people least expect to find them. This is not the case with your You-Know-What. People expect it out in plain sight because they think you're stupid.

Behind Furniture. It sometimes works here. Except it gets uncovered eventually by the maid when she's vacuuming, or the kids when they're playing Vasco da Gama. Both squeal on you immediately, of course. So you plead the Fifth. Your reasoning:

they can't pin it on me if it's not fresh. Only one problem: for human beings there is no statute of limitations on You-Know-What.

In Closets. Same as above.

In short, You-Know-What can't be hidden permanently. Not even Houdini tried it, so don't bother trying it or persisting with it yourself.

Try this next time: ask to go outside. Scratch the door, whine, or hit the knob with your nose. You won't believe how happy this will make your people. Because the first stage of Boot Camp is over and they haven't enjoyed it any more than you.

You're Housebroken.

II. Basic Training and Obedience

INTRODUCTION: LEARNING ENGLISH (GREEK, OR WHATEVER)

The second stage of Boot Camp is learning English, Greek, or whatever else your people speak. During Housebreaking you were taught your first four words: your name, plus *no, bad,* and *dog.* But these were little more than prohibitive yells and screams at the time than anything else. Now you are about to learn your first four specific human concepts, a thorough understanding of and obedience to which are the cornerstones of getting along with human beings. Come, Sit, Stay, and Heel.

A. COME!

1. LEARNING IT

GLOSSARY 1

COME *vi.* 1. To advance toward a human being calling your name. 2. To arrive as a result of moving, or making progress. 3. To move into view, appear.

Most human beings, even if they haven't read Barbara Wodehouse, will teach you how to come in a similar way. Now we will learn it over again together. Put yourself in the following hypothetical situation. . . .

You have been Adopted by a typical American couple with kids. Frank and Sheila Johnson. You are three months old, a German shepherd-Labrador retriever cross, and the Johnsons have named you Boomer, short for Boomerang, because of how you love to retrieve things, especially Frank's wingtips. Otherwise, you are paper trained, almost Housebroken. It is a Saturday morning now when Frank and Sheila take you out into the yard with this equipment: fifty-foot lead, choke collar, and a box of dog yummies.

The kids watch from the back porch as Sheila sits you down at one end of the yard while Frank unravels the lead at the other. When he gets there, after his wife slips the choke over your head and snaps on the lead, he crouches in a catcher's position, smiles at you, and claps his hands.

"Boomer, come!"

Cocking your head, the first thing that occurs to you is to run for Frank like usual; but, on second thought, this seems too obvious. Also, why is this rope on your neck? You glance at Sheila, but Sheila is playing Switzerland. So you just sit down.

Now Frank claps twice and gives the lead a tug, "Boomer, *come!*"

Feeling the choke suddenly, you take a step back. It gets snugger. You look at Sheila again, eyes slightly out.

"I think you're scaring him, honey," she calls to Frank. "Give him some slack. And don't sound so mean."

"Who's sounding mean?!"

After they consult another minute, Frank kneels down on the grass and, with a very patient smile, claps his hands again and gives the lead a good one this time.

"Boomer, I said *come!*"

Now having even less idea what this word could mean, only that the lead has become a guy wire and you are having some trouble breathing, you reel back.

"Don't pull him, Frank!"

"I'm not pulling. *He's* pulling!"

Later that morning, after the tenth or twentieth try, the lesson ends in one of three ways:

SCENARIO 1

Thinking you have at last figured out the meaning of come, all at once you drop to the grass, tail and ears down, squirming.

Sheila hugs you and gives you a yummie.

Frank looks at her incredulously from the other end of the lawn. "What the hell did you give him a yummie for?!"

"He's crying, poor baby."

Frank flings down the lead. "Fantastic. Now you've got him all confused."

SCENARIO 2

You turn into a mustang, Frank turns into a cowboy. Sheila and the kids immediately join your side, and it turns into a tug of war, four against one.

"You can't force him!" cries Sheila after she wins.

"What am I supposed to do—say 'Boomer, *please*?'" fumes Frank. "The stupid mutt's got to learn to come sooner or later. What's so complicated about it?"

"It's not, if you do it the right way."

"Oh, fine. *I'm* the moron. You teach him!"

At which point Sheila takes over. Now you have another few alternatives. If you come for her, Frank will boil over. If you don't, she will get annoyed and you will lose your only ally; and Frank, vindicated, will take over again, his good mood restored. If, after a month or two of this, you still aren't coming—for Frank or Sheila—they will buy Barbara Wodehouse, take you to obedience school, or get rid of you.

SCENARIO 3

That morning or another, options exhausted, you start crawling in their direction to give yourself some slack on the lead. When you get to the other end, everybody goes wild. "Good boy, Boomer!"

Even though your windpipe has felt better, they shower you with yummies. It's what humans call positive reinforcement.

Of the three scenarios listed, the last is recommended, though it may seem like the most illogical at the time.

2. THE FIVE KINDS OF DOGS

After puppyhood, people stop accepting a dog's excuses for not Coming. Such as that you still don't know the definition of *Come*. Or that when you hear your owner call, "Here, Boomer!" you assume he's just letting you know where he is in case you're interested, or that he's paging some other dog in the neighborhood by the same name. Or perhaps you happen to be busy at the moment: relieving yourself, baptizing trees, chasing bad cars, socializing with friends, treeing a mailman, mulching a flowerbed, straightening out a cat, working a cocktail party, or having sex for the first time in years. Or, after you are finished with this pressing business and hear "Boomer, *Come!!*" you now proceed in the opposite direction because you know your owner intends to kick your ass in.

In short, don't underestimate the importance, in the human mind, of Coming when you are called—stat, no excuses. From the beginning of time people have decided what kind of dog you are according to whether you Come, and under what conditions you Come—as follows:

B. SIT! STAY! HEEL!

1. LEARNING IT

The last of the Big Four human commands and of Basic Training itself are the sixth, seventh, and eighth words: *Sit! Stay!* and *Heel!*

And, again, the first step in mastering them is to learn the definitions.

KIND OF DOG	DESCRIPTION
1. A Good Dog	A dog that comes when he is called—immediately, no matter what.
2. A Stupid Dog	A dog that comes when he is called—strictly by coincidence.
3. An Opportunist	A dog that comes when he is called—if there's something in it for him (yummies, leftovers, sofa privileges, etc.). But otherwise doesn't bother.
4. A Hedonist	A dog that comes when he is called—if it's no inconvenience.
5. A Sonuvabitch	A dog that comes when he is called—never. As a simple matter of policy.

GLOSSARY 2

Sit, *vi.* 1. To rest with the hindquarters lowered onto a supporting surface.

Stay, *vi.* 1. To remain in a given place. 2. To stop moving; cease, halt. 3. To wait, pause. 4. To hold on, endure.

Heel, *vi.* 1. To follow at the heels (of a human).

Just looking at this Glossary, many more of you will be tempted to become Stupid Dogs, Opportunists, Hedonists, or Sonuvabitches. This is because you can already predict the following situations, if you haven't been in them yet. . . .

- You are begging at the table, the kids teasing you with ice cream, cake, and cookies. The floor around your paws is a skating rink of drool. You look around for a second, you are about to nail the entire cake . . . Suddenly a grown-up steps in. *"Sit!"*

- You are in heat. Your boyfriend across the street is chained. Finally you eat through the fence in your backyard, your body is halfway through it . . . then your owner barges out. *"Stay!"*

- You are on a walk with your people . . . When all of a sudden for the first time you spot the neighbor's cat on the flats, no cover in sight. *"Heel!"*

At times like these you wonder if a human being could do any of these three things themselves.

III. Tricks

Boot Camp is over!

But you are the last to know. In fact, for some time you have wondered why you let yourself get drafted. The service seems to be all drills and no R and R. You think Boot Camp will never end.

Then suddenly and without warning one night, your owner pushes his chair back from the dinner table, lifts a huge, juicy piece of New York fat off his plate, and, smiling, says:

"Beg."

Word 9. What could it possibly mean? you ask yourself.

GLOSSARY 3

Beg, *vi.* 1. To solicit alms. 2. To make a plea for in a way that is earnest, humble, and designed to stir pity.

Eyes glazed on the New York fat, stalactites forming at the corners of your mouth, you raise one paw without realizing it.

"That's adorable," says another human at the table. "Give it to him, for heaven's sake, Frank. After all he's been through, he deserves it."

Frank drops the New York in your mouth. "Good boy."

Word 10. The last vocabulary in Basic. *Good.*

People love you after all. They are not sadists.

The next thing you know, they are teaching you your first Trick. They keep saying "Good" while giving you leftover cheesecake.

What's come over them?

Abruptly it dawns on you. You have graduated from Boot Camp: it's Trick time. You are on the threshold of a brand-new life!

But before you lose control, here are a few tips about Tricks:

Unlike the Big Four, Tricks are optional. Extras. Very few human beings will force a Trick on you. So, in spite of initial post Boot Camp, I-love-everybody élan, try not to get into the habit of doing your Tricks for free. It sets a bad precedent. Think of Tricks as your only way of compensating for everything else you do without charge. Also, many of the old begging standbys—sitting up, speaking, rolling over—involve, if you think about it, making a fool of yourself. And there is no reason you should agree to this without payment. Granted, it might be necessary when you are just starting out to do a complimentary promo routine or two— just to let the public know what you've got. But after that, turn professional as soon as possible and don't budge toward the hoops without a yummie advance.

Above all, remember you can collect on Tricks while you are learning, long before they're perfected. That's the beauty of them. In fact, they can be amateur, even bungled. What matters to us human beings most is effort, desire to please, and a cute expression. You'll get almost more yummies and hugs than you can handle just for this.

Once you have a small repertoire together, you are ready to tour. Cocktail parties, barbecues, open houses. And don't worry, your owner probably won't stop you. House guests love Tricks. That's entertainment. Especially after they've had a few martinis. You, however, remain cold sober and ready to sweep the hors d'oeuvres.

III

TERRITORY

INTRODUCTION

Now that you are Adopted and have gone through Boot Camp, it is time to stake out some turf. Territory.

Territory is important to everybody because it is the only place we can pursue life's five most important activities at leisure and with least fear of repercussion: eating, socializing, mating, having puppies, and going to the bathroom. These activities are not the same on foreign ground. Especially the last three.

In short, Territory is the key ingredient to well-being, self-respect, and general security. These are life's three most important commodities—for all creatures, not just dogs.

Furthermore, the main difference between a loiterer, a passer-through, a maverick, a rootless lowlife and a creature of substance (whether it be a dog, a human being, or anybody else) is: a deed on a piece of real estate.

Therefore, Territory has been the common basis of most bloodletting in animal history. It has even caused many misunderstandings between human beings and you dogs, in spite of

our alliance. Thus, it needs careful scrutiny and reexamination in the following categories: Staking It Out, Border Control, Infiltration, and Imperialism.

I. Staking It Out

A. THE PROBLEM

When a human being sees a piece of property he likes—whether it be two hundred acres in the country, a parcel in the suburbs, a brownstone in the city—he has to put some money down and start *escrow*, before he can actually move in and start eating, socializing, mating, having a family, and going to the bathroom. Escrow involves a good deal of paperwork and financial suspense. Money is the most important ingredient. It is also made of paper, but real. Think of it as a certificate redeemable by so many bones or yummies.

The human being who's leaving the piece of property tries to get as many bones and yummies as possible from the human being coming in. The latter tries to expend as few as possible. The process is overseen by a number of other human beings who get a cut of the yummies for their trouble. There is the person who lists the Territory, drives you to it, and makes the deal look good for everybody. There is the person who lends you the yummies for the sale in exchange for twice as many from you over a period of time. There is the person who insures all this, the paperwork and arithmetic person, and the person who goes over all the paperwork and arithmetic, making sure everything is above-board, or—in the event that it isn't—the person who takes everyone to court and makes large withdrawals from their yummies accounts for material damages and emotional distress.

That's approximately how human beings Stake Out Territory.

Modern ones. It's actually a good deal more complicated than this, but we have simplified matters for the sake of brevity.

Now contrast this with your own procedure.

You see a piece of property you like. Piss all around the perimeter. Possibly kick some ass in the process. Then move in.

The Veni, Vidi, Vici Approach. V^3.

V^3 is the way human beings used to handle most of their real estate transactions. (In fact, the coiner of the phrase took over all of Gaul that way.) In certain parts of the world, especially places that are called "underdeveloped," they still use this technique.

There is something to be said for the V^3 Stakeout, not the least of which is that it cuts out the real estate agent and escrow.

Indeed, many modern humans—particularly those who for one reason or another find their resources continually exhausted by groceries—view the old V^3 Territorial Imperative with wistfulness and nostalgia. They imagine themselves taking a drive out to Brentwood with their suitcase; parking in front of a dream house; getting out; relieving themselves at strategic points along the fenceline; then knocking on the door and asking the maid for the man of the house; kicking his ass when he appears; then simply moving in.

How easy it would be. Utopian. Except for one thing.

The Police.

This is the Problem.

They usually arrive before you can get your bag unpacked and your swimming trunks on.

The same problem confronts you dogs on a V^3 Stakeout. Animal Control officers are the Police. Their job is to take care of those of you who don't know or refuse to accept the difference between Scarsdale and the Yukon, or John Cheever and Jack London.

B. THE SOLUTION

Now we are ready to introduce a modified, two-prong Stake-Out policy which accords with human beings, modern ones, and will help you avoid misunderstandings with them down the road when securing Territory.

1. PISS, BUT NOT ON EVERYTHING

This applies to you guy dogs, notably those of you who haven't been fixed yet. In that regard, this section may help you delay or escape that eventuality. (Also, see Chapter VII, "Getting Fixed: Prevention.")

Bitches, you usually have no problem in this area—pissing on everything—so bear with us for a few moments.

Guys—first a general note. You have already learned during House Training that human beings don't feel the same about your product as you do. They believe that it belongs outside. Furthermore, many of them don't sympathize with your need, even when outside, to go in more than one spot, or to make a *production* out of it. The smelling, fur and tail up, the twirls, clawing the grass is considered unnecessary. To some, it is even disgusting. But we try to make allowance for it, hoping you will make allowance for us as follows:

Don't just go out and nail every trunk, fencepost, and other vertical in sight after graduating from Basic. Because there are certain items people don't like to see you relieve yourself on with regularity, for Stake-Out purposes.

LIST: WHAT NOT TO PISS ON

a. The Grass. Especially if you see your owner spend evenings and weekends sprinkling it, applying Turf Builder, etc.
b. Lawn Ornaments. A jockey. Deer. Geese. Flamingos. Snowmen.
c. The Mailbox.
d. Important Trees, Shrubs, and Flowers.
e. Car Tires. (If, however, you still can't resist, work the far side of the auto, make it quick, and avoid the hubcap.)
f. House and Outbuildings.
g. Patio Furniture.
h. Sporting Equipment, Garden Equipment, The Kids' Bicycles.
i. A Human Being. Especially one wearing cuffs, or loafers without socks.

2. REDEFINE TERRITORY

After your first Stakeout, most of you will have this thought:

"I'm not in British Columbia."

Here is a breakdown of your population according to a recent demographic survey. It covers only the U.S. Numbers elsewhere—Africa, Pakistan, Latin America, etc.—are more sobering.

Consulting the Dog Demography graph, note which of the five groups you fall into, have formerly fallen into, or acquaintances and relatives of yours fall into. Those of you on a farm or who own acreage in the suburbs with a swimming pool or other recreational facilities—count your blessings.

The other 78 percent of you must make do with considerably less. City dogs in particular. You are lucky if you have access to a park or playground. Guys must settle for just a tree everybody and his brother has hit a hundred times already that morning. Bitches get a patch of grass. Nor does the average pro walker allow you a second's free reign in these areas.

So this is the reality. Some of you are becoming depressed. Getting Adopted wasn't easy, nor was Boot Camp. Now, just when

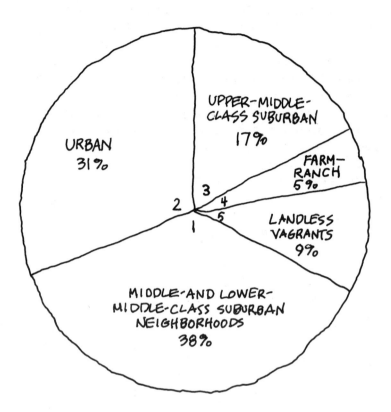

DOG DEMOGRAPHY

1. Includes those of you living in trailer parks, renewal projects, developments, and military and industrial installations, with lots down to 75′ × 100′.
2. No lot at all. You have to go to the bathroom in the street.
3. Parcels ranging from one acre to one quarter acre, depending on zoning.
4. Ten acres and up.
5. Those of you who are in-between situations. Traveling in rural packs. Suburban gangs. Solo, crossing state lines without ID. Or presently residing in the pound, someone's crawlspace, under their porch; working the back of Burger King, Taco Bell, Holiday Inn, etc.

you are ready to collect on your dues and claim some real estate, you find yourself on a divorcée's leash, Lexington Avenue; or chained to the young married couple's clothesline in a mobile home park; perhaps tied in the back of a single guy's pickup; in chainlink behind the widower's condominium; or possibly locked in the family garage, laundry room, or toolshed.

But it's not as bad as it sounds as long as you Redefine Territory, claiming kingdoms in the vastness of your little things. Your doghouse. Your lawn, no matter how small. And your personal possessions: your collar, your lead, your dinner bowl, your bed, your toys, your stick, your bone.

II. Border Control

Now that you have Staked Out your Territory without relieving yourself on everything, and found a thousand acres of British Columbia in your own backyard, or an elm off Fifty-second Street, you are ready for a new and better kind of Border Control.

The first thing to learn here is . . .

A. THE POWER OF DEED AND THE IMPORTANCE OF SHARING WITH HUMAN BEINGS

STORYTIME

There was once a piece of Territory in the suburbs which three different creatures thought they owned.

The first creature was Bob. Bob was a big black and orange potato beetle with huge jaws, powerful antennae, and terrible barbed legs. He lived under a large brown rock in the backyard next to a pile of garden clippings from the edges of which sprung

towering dandelions. His domain stretched for as far as his eye could see from the tallest of these, and there was not a creature in it that didn't run from him: ant, caterpillar, grub, chigger, roach, weevil, millipede, centipede, grasshopper, daddy longlegs, or wolf spider. Two months old, Bob was in the prime of his life, a summer day lasted a year for him, and he foresaw no end to his dominion. He had a wife, Edith; many tenacious girlfriends; and his sons were so abundant he made a policy of eating them to prevent coups d'état.

The second creature was Sidney, a gray squirrel who lived in the huge oak tree which overshadowed Bob's rock. Sidney could fly forty feet out of his front door onto the back of a lizard in the neighboring sugar maple. He was the size of a small airplane. His claws were razor sharp. His tail fearsomely bristly. And his teeth halved acorns without effort. His territory extended as far as he could see from the hundred-foot main tower of the oak, and not a creature in this wide domain—mouse, mole, shrew, chipmunk, lizard, toad, salamander, blue jay, robin—failed to shudder when pronouncing Sidney's name. Sidney had a wife, Angela. He kept an assortment of infatuations in nearby trees. And he enjoyed his twins, Demian and Emory. At four, Sidney was in his prime, a summer day lasted a week for him, and he too saw no end to his dominion in the yard.

The third creature was a human being named Frank Johnson. Frank was 5 feet 10, 175 pounds, his nails were clipped, his teeth in good condition, he jogged on weekends, and he was an insurance adjuster. He had just bought the yard, and it included, in addition to the rock and the oak tree, a three-bedroom, two-bath split-level. The price was $105,000; escrow had closed; he and his family had moved in last week and were now eating, socializing, mating, and going to the bathroom on the property without interference from the police. Frank's family included: his wife, Sheila, thirty-four; his two children, Frank, Jr., nine, and Sally, six; and his dog, Boomer, a lab-shepherd mix, one. At thirty-six, Frank himself was in the prime of his life, a year lasted exactly a year for him, his job was secure, and he didn't expect foreclosure.

So, whose yard really was it: Bob's, Sidney's, or Frank's?

It is the first Saturday morning on his new property and Frank is contentedly strolling his lawn with Boomer when all at once he stops and stares down into the grass, his smile turning to a frown.

"Sonuvabitch," he says, "look at that."

Boomer's eyes join Frank's. All around his paws he sees thousands of little things eating, socializing, etc., in Frank's grass. Suddenly his master turns toward the kitchen window.

"Sheila, there are frigging bugs all over our lawn! Keep the kids in!"

Moments later Boomer watches Frank—now in a ball cap, a respirator, and with a metal tank strapped to his back—spraying a perfumed white water over the yard, shouting under his mask as he marches.

"HaHA! How's that, you sonsuvbitches? Eat it!"

At this point Bob is a short distance from his rock terminating an invading wolf spider, and just as he feels the sticky dew drizzling over him and his victim, he looks up and, seeing something tall as the Empire State Building race past, in a respirator, remarks to himself:

"Strange weather."

Then he goes on about his business, devouring the wolf.

A half hour later Frank, enjoying a cigarette and some iced tea on the porch with Boomer, is gazing out over the lawn with a violent, apocalyptical grin. Feet away Bob, experiencing tachycardia, shortness of breath, and double vision, keels into the portulaca onto his back, and gasps: "What the hell was *in* that spider?" Then, as his legs buckle inward and the blood drains from his head, he vaguely hears a shriek from the direction of his house—Edith.

"Bob! Good God. Bo-o-b-b!!"

After lunch Frank reappears in his yard with Boomer, his smile growing out of the wonderful silence which hangs over it. Suddenly, however, under the dense shade of the oak, the smile turns to a frown, and again he turns toward the kitchen.

"The lawn's not getting any light back here, Sheila!"

While Frank is inside making a phone call, Sidney, a late riser, makes his way down to the yard for a leisurely brunch, and finds there two things. A sticky white film covering a billion upside-down bugs. And, next to the rock, a black and orange potato beetle large as a rolled Volkswagon, with the body of a woman flung on top of it. Bob and Edith. But of course Sidney has no idea this is Bob and Edith. So he casually proceeds with his morning acorns. Shortly he is back in his tree, lying on his veranda, experiencing vertigo and an upset stomach. And, in this condition, he falls fast asleep.

All at once, hearing an explosive roar at the base of his tree, Sidney awakens. Below he sees a human being in a hard hat and an orange shirt with a beaver on it, holding a screaming metal apparatus to the trunk, white flakes flying everywhere. Then he hears a shriek.

"Sidney! Good God. SidneyYYY!"

This, followed by a thunderous crash—himself, Angela, and the twins in the center of it, airborne.

Boomer is now sitting on the porch with Frank, the family, and the tree service man, bright light streaming down over the lawn.

"You've got some sun now and a little cord wood, too," observes the tree man.

Frank nods. Then gazes into the distance. "Hey, look at that big squirrel over on the rock, kids."

But just as they do, Sidney jumps over the fence and disappears into the woods forever, leaving Bob under the oak tree, and the new owners on the porch looking mystified.

MORAL

Escrow, deed of trust, amortization schedule may seem like nonsense to everybody except people, but don't make us prove their importance. Insect spray and the tree man are only the beginning. We haven't even mentioned bazookas, the National Guard, SWAT, or the Strategic Defense Initiative. We don't want to scare you dogs.

Just learn to share the yard with us.

B. THE FIVE SCHOOLS OF BORDER CONTROL

Now that you have learned to share Territory with human beings, it's time to examine the Schools of Border Control. As you may know, there are five.

1. I'M-OK-YOU'RE-OK SCHOOL
Members: Retrievers (except Chesapeakes), Irish setters, pointers, weimaraners, otter hounds, German shorthaireds.

Policy: When a thief, kidnapper, or homicidal maniac happens by the property, assume he's a friend of the family and let him into the house for a reunion with Frank, Sheila, and the kids if he passes the secret test: throws the ball for you first.

2. WALL-OF-SOUND SCHOOL
Members: Schnauzers, cockers, toy poodles, dachshunds, Chihuahuas, shelties, terriers, Pekingese, pugs, Shih Tzus. Generally anybody little who figures the best way of compensating for this is by making a huge racket.

Policy: If anything approaches the Border—you don't necessarily even have to see it—start barking like crazy and don't stop no matter what. If whatever it is still keeps coming or actually appears, either head for cover and hit new decibles, or charge its shoes piranha-style—then fall back, regroup, and repeat until your turf is cleared.

3. MAKE-MY-DAY SCHOOL

Members: German shepherds, Dobermans, pit bulls, Rottweilers, mastiffs, spitzes, chowchows, Pomeranians. Generally anybody with an important bone, fed up, in heat, or trying to get to somebody in heat.

Policy: If a visitor happens by without an armed guard or without your owner as a personal chaperon, assume that they are a blood donor.

4. ENIGMATIC SCHOOL

Members: Chesapeakes, Newfoundlands, borzois, Great Pyrenees, Great Danes, malamutes, Samoyeds, huskies, anything part wolf, or schizoid mutts.

Policy: As soon as somebody steps a millimeter past your fenceline—a real estate agent, encyclopedia salesperson, a dry cleaner, a pervert, whoever—neither encouraging them or discouraging them, track their progress with your pupils, not your entire head. When they are within range and reach out their hand and say, "Hey, poochie, do you bite?" either answer them by amputating or by ignoring them—depending on your mood that day.

5. THE YELLOW SCHOOL

Members: Anybody chicken, shy, or just fixed.
Policy: Whatever you see—hide.

So, these are the Five Old Schools of Border control. Now the new.

The important thing here, since you are sharing Territory with a person, is to follow his/her own B.C. Policy. This is often easier than you think. For example, if you are a German shepherd or any other traditional member of School 3, your owner probably doesn't object to a Make-My-Day attitude, and under certain circumstances will be upset if you fail to make hamburger out of a stranger, or to at least give the impression you're about to. You can be sure of this if your owner has any signs around saying, BEWARE OF DOG, TRESPASSERS WILL BE EATEN, etc.—even if you are just a Chihuahua in Beverly Hills. On the other hand, if you are a retriever, chances are your owner—more concerned about getting sued than with the possibility Charles Manson may drop by— prefers your open-door policy. In the case of you Lhasas, shelties, Pekingese, and so on, though your Wall of Sound may sometimes annoy your people, they probably like the chance it gives them to go out, see who's there, and become part of the B.C. decision-making process.

But what people would really like to see from you in this New Border Control is a judicious combination of the Five Schools, varying according to the kind of person who appears at the door.

C. THE TEN KINDS OF HUMAN BEINGS AND HOW TO HANDLE THEM

Each of the following entries representing one of the ten kinds of human beings is accompanied by an index number. This number indicates how you should correctly Border Control that kind of person under ordinary circumstances.

1. I'm OK, You're OK: wag and lick.
2. Wall of Sound: bark and attack footwear.
3. Make My Day: hamburger.
4. Enigmatic: review options, then amputate or ignore.
5. Yellow: hide.

Also, from now on rather than continually using the impersonal terms *your owner* or *your people*, the names *Frank* or *Sheila*, or their children *Frank Jr.* or *Sally* will be used instead, though of course these names are arbitrary and refer to no humans in particular but generally to people who own dogs or love them.

1. FRIENDS, RELATIVES, AND NEIGHBORS—1

Immediately after Getting Adopted, draw up a complete list of your family's friends, relatives, and neighbors. All these people are OK. Not that your family necessarily likes all relatives and neighbors, or is particularly thrilled when some of them appear at the door or the fenceline. But complications arise when they act like they are less than thrilled, or when you—picking up on these vibrations and with the intention of being helpful—pull a number 3 on your owner's mother-in-law in the backyard one day, or on a next-door neighbor who happens to be an attorney. So, play it safe: wag and lick whenever your family's friends, relatives, or neighbors drop by the Territory.

2. CHILDREN—1

Again, as far as you dogs are concerned, kids can be heaven or hell. There is almost no middle ground with a kid. He is either being your best buddy or he is pulling your tail or ears, making believe you are his entry in the Belmont, playing Monkey-in-the Middle with his friends, with you as It, exploring the very limits of your sanity, via his peanut butter sandwich, a single one of his corn chips, or a crumb off his Oreo. Certain children may do just about everything you can imagine that—even on a good day and even if you are a twelve-year-old Irish setter—makes you want to strip their bones.

But don't. Even if you have never seen the kid before in your life, you're in your own yard, on your chain, minding your own business, with a bone from Frank or Sheila's New York. Human beings don't understand extenuating circumstances like these. We feel the same way about our kids as you do your puppies. Lick them. Be nice. No matter what.

3. SOLICITORS—2 OR (IN RARE CASES)—4

These are people who come to your property selling cosmetics, encyclopedias, insurance (especially personal liability or accidental death and dismemberment policies), vacuums and other household accessories, and so on. You don't have to know much about the products other than that your owner, if he doesn't already have them, probably isn't interested. So when you see someone enter the drive in an Aries, Escort, Cordoba, or old Toyota, carrying a sample case, and dressed in a Sears 2-for-1 suit—bark.

After Frank, Sheila, or one of the kids joins you at the door, listen to the pitch with them objectively. Then, through a combination of Psychic Smell, ESP (see Chapter VIII, The Supernatural, "Occult powers"), and common sense, decide if your people are interested in the new Avon, World Book, or noncontingency dismemberment clause. If not, and the solicitor is slow on the intake, resume or increase barking. If he starts crowding the door then, interest *him* in the dismemberment policy: i.e., look Enigmatic, with some gumline.

4. JEHOVAH'S WITNESSES—5

If you see two human beings materialize in the drive on foot, bicycle, or via an ordinary-looking sedan; wearing Montgomery Ward white shirts and snap-on ties; introduce themselves by their first names at the front door while completely ignoring you no matter what you are doing; and then ask your owner a seemingly ordinary question, but which includes anything like ". . . blood of the lamb . . . ," ". . . only 25 cents . . . ," ". . . Armageddon . . . ," or something else you have never heard from the Avon lady or All State man, then stop whatever you are doing—1, 2, 3, or 4—and go to the garage. 5. This is religion. Don't get involved in it. It has to do with the salvation of Frank and Sheila's soul. A subject on which human beings widely and energetically differ.

This will become clear to you when you overhear Frank's response to the question an instant later, from the garage.

A slam of the door. Or . . .

"Sheila, would you mind coming out here for a sec, honey?" Or . . .

"Forget it. I'm Catholic." Or . . .

He invites the two in for some juice.

But, no matter what happens, *keep under cover—5*. For people, there is only one bigger bone than Territory. Religion. Don't come out of the garage till you hear Frank close the door, go back to the den, and turn the Niners game back on.

5. PUBLIC SERVANTS AND UTILITYMEN—1

Mailmen (including UPS and Federal Express). Electric man. Water and sewer man. AT&T guy.

Over the years you dogs have pulled 2's, 3's, and 4's on these professionals almost more than anybody else. They don't deserve it. You may not use the phone, the stereo, or the bathroom too often, or get mail as much as you would like, but that doesn't go for everybody in your family.

6. DELIVERY, TRADES, MAINTENANCE PEOPLE, ETC.—1

Dry cleaner, milkman, FTD, garbageman, paperboy, plumber, carpenter, electrician, gardener, tree trimmer, pool man, lawn service guy, maid, babysitter.

Theoretically, they wouldn't be around unless Frank called them. Be polite.

7. REAL ESTATE AGENTS—1 OR 4

Many of you—especially pits, Dobies, Rottweilers, etc.—share an opinion about Real Estate Agents. To some extent it is justified. Their business is to sell your property out from under you without considering how you feel about it. And because there are many yummie certificates at stake for your owner, you'll have to wag your tail. Your own recourse will be to give the agent an Enigmatic look—4—in the event that he's thinking of pulling a fast one on Frank and Sheila during escrow. In the meantime, all you can do is go out and baptize his Le Baron.

8. THE VET—1, 2, 3, 4, OR 5

It all depends. (Also, see Chapter VII, "Backing Off a Vet")

9. ANIMAL CONTROL OFFICER—1 OR 5

Act innocent, be charming. Dematerialize. Or head for British Columbia. (For details, see next feature: "Fate of the Biter.")

10. LOITERERS, CRIMINALS, PERVERTS—3

The preceding nine recommendations may have you frustrated, suggesting self-control and prudence. At last here you have a group of human beings that allows you freedom of expression. Before you nail somebody, though, you want to be quite sure about ID. In the case of a loiterer: that your suspect isn't just the pool man, gardener, or paperboy, waiting to collect, without his hair combed. In guarding against criminals, one must ensure that the person breaking into your house in the middle of the night isn't just Frank, locked out by Sheila. The guy peeping through the bathroom window just a real estate agent on a multiple listing.

D. BITING PEOPLE: THE ADVISABILITY OF DETENTE

1. GENERAL REMARKS

It may surprise you dogs, but most human beings are scared of getting bitten by you. Even just a cocker. This probably dates back to our caveman days and the genetic memory of being chased by wolves, coyotes, hyenas, then overtaken, dragged down, and eaten alive by an entire pack. More recently it traces back to when we were kids: there's hardly one of us who doesn't remember being terrorized by one of you in our neighborhood; we had nightmares about you catching us inside your fence one day. It wouldn't have been so bad if we thought you would just trample us like an elephant, or carry us away like a huge bird. No, it was the thought of you having us for dinner, going at us with those tremendous white teeth—that was the thing.

So, generally, animals with a reputation for biting—snakes, crocodiles, eels, sharks, barracuda, piranha, gila monsters, saber-toothed tigers, vampire bats, and you dogs—have the greatest grip on the human imagination. Even just a little spider. Many rational, two-hundred-pound men will flee a spider as if it were a full-grown tyrannosaur. The thought here is not simply of being bitten, but of being held down viselike by eight hairy legs while the spider's jagged beak nurses our veins.

Objectively speaking, however, the sensation of being bitten—short of losing a limb in the process, or actually being Osterized by you dogs like, say, Jezebel in the book of Kings—is probably not as bad as we think. But since few people are ready to field test such a theory, human prejudice will most likely remain intact on the subject for the foreseeable future, and you dogs will continue to bear the brunt. To give you a preview of what is meant here by "brunt," and why we have recommended Biting People in only one case—bona fide Loiterers, Criminals, or Perverts—

2. FEATURE: FATE OF THE BITER—YOU
A Tale with Another Moral, and a Few Suggestions

Even if biting a person has never crossed your mind, imagine the following. . . .

You are lying out on the front porch one morning, on the lawn, in your doghouse, wherever, when you see a late model Econoline pull up to your curb. The windows are steel reinforced, and on the driver's door appears the city seal with two words under it: *Animal Control.* As adrenaline travels from your chest cavity to your paws, and your neck hair goes vertical, you slowly raise yourself up on an elbow, pupils dilating on the Ford, and think:

"Jesus H. What do I do now?"

All right.

1. Don't Panic.

   Now, try to remember: Have you recently done something not recommended in the preceding section? Like to Frank's mother-in-law, the kid with the peanut butter sandwich, a Jehovah's Witness, the Century 21 man?

   Don't waste your time with Yes, buts. Yes, but I thought they were loitering, perverted, whatever. At the inquest you won't even be called to the stand. You can't talk, and people don't have a lot of respect for your opinion anyway, much less your rationalizations.

   All right, then, the answer to the question is a simple, unmitigated yes—you did bite somebody. Now what do you do?

2. Quietly and before anybody gets out of the van, TAKE COVER—5. Like wherever you went during House Training after you'd had an accident.

Now, while keeping an eye on the Ford from here, try to remember something else: How did the person you attacked leave your yard? On his own steam? Or on a stretcher? If you are a schnauzer, you probably have nothing to worry about. If you are a Doberman, pit bull, shepherd, bull mastiff, and you see the officer exit the van now dressed in an astronaut or hockey goalie outfit and carrying a leash, muzzle, and/or traq gun—you may have a problem.

OK, no matter who you are, let's assume the worst anyway. A real estate agent pulled into your yard; minutes later some neighbors pulled him out, prone; you took a snooze and hacked around with your ball for a while; then the Ford arrived.

Now, as you watch the Animal Control officer in the Apollo suit inch into your yard, consider your options and the probable results.

a. SURRENDER

If you come out with your paws up, the A.C. officer will be relieved. But he still has to drive you downtown, muzzled. You will spend the next days or weeks in a cell next to other biters. Meanwhile, one of several things takes place. The person you bit sues your people for all their yummy certificates or assets, including your house. A judge decides under what conditions you can return home. Or he sentences you to the decompression chamber. The d.c. chamber is a closet people suck all the air out of, with you in it. When you come out, you're not in any condition to bite humans, ever again.

b. FIGHT

A Rambo routine may work with the first A.C. officer. But there are more where he came from. So, heroics just guarantee the d.c. chamber in the long run. No last-minute reprieve from the governor. And if Warner Brothers picks up your option, it will be posthumously.

c. FLIGHT

Call of the Wild, Cujo, Lassie Come Home. The fate of
fugitives has been overglorified. First comes the APB. Then
photos of you in the post office. Then the life of a stray, a
beggar, a rootless maverick. The bottom line: only Lassie
gets home again.

Moral of the Tale

Don't bite people. They'll make you pay.

E. EPILOGUE: BULLYING CATS

So what now are you left with? Can any stranger just traipse onto
your property with impunity, your paws tied? Would divine justice
allow such a thing?

Of course not.

Right after God made you in Genesis, He said to Himself:

"Now let's make something that will give this dog a well-earned relief and mission on his property. A creature slinky; deviously indirect, aloof, self-satisfied; finicky, prissy, can't stand dirt; relieves itself in a box, eats fish, preys on lizards and rodents, electrifies entire human neighborhoods with its mating cries; which creeps through the dog's yard constantly as if it is infinitely superior; in short, a creature which offends his deepest sensibilities, convictions, and instincts . . .

"THE CAT!"

Then God, satisfied that he was inaugurating Creation's greatest rivalry, mincing His hands with zest, continued:

"All right, let's make the dog bigger. But the cat can climb trees."

Finally, on the decisive issue—SPEED—He exclaimed:

"In any given backyard, let's make it even steven!"

So, ever since that time, as you know, you dogs have been treeing cats. And, as you also know, there is only one thing better than treeing a cat.

That's beating him to the tree.

You can vent every territorial frustration you have had to endure with human beings until now by just kicking some cat ass.

III. Infiltration and Imperialism

A. INNOCENCE AND DISCRETION

The first step in a successful Lawn Infiltration involves the use of common sense. To get onto somebody else's lawn, you have to be able to get off your own. Which means you can't be chained to it or penned on it. How, then, do you avoid lockup in the first place?

Generally, by being a good dog. Specifically, by not giving your people any idea that you intend to Infiltrate Lawns. Bitches, this will be easier for you than guys, even fixed ones. That's one of the many beauties of being a bitch. You seldom have to leave the lawn. So people chain you up less. Ten guys are in chains to every one bitch. Anyway, look innocent, whoever you are.

Looking innocent, however, is a waste of time if, as soon as you cut out, you throw discretion to the wind and get nailed.

Nothing irritates a dog owner more than a call like this. . . .

"Hello, Frank, Frank Johnson?"

"Speaking."

"John Stansbury, your new neighbor next door. Your dog, Boomer, is in my yard."

"That can't be. I just saw him here, right out in back."

"Well, he's not now. He's in my wife's flowerbed. I've had to put my bitch in the garage."

"Is your bitch in heat?"

"She may be coming in, yes. But this is the tenth time Boomer has been over here since you moved in. I can't have this anymore."

Full details of what may transpire after Frank hangs up will come in the next chapter's Storytime—"The AWOLer." Suffice it to say for now that you get chained to your yard, at least.

In conclusion: 1. Look Innocent at home. 2. Be Discreet when you are out.

But what is Discretion?

B. TIMING, AND SOME GOOD JUDGMENT

Timing, and Some Good Judgment, is the better part of Discretion.

If you intend to colonize a suburban neighborhood, to amass an empire, even a modest one, time your Lawn Infiltration in these stages, using Some Good Judgment. . . .

1. LEAVE THE HOUSE when nobody is around to see you leave the house. Or when there is the *least chance* of them seeing you leave, i.e., when they are: a. Asleep. b. Going to the bathroom. c. Sick. d. Watching an important TV program. e. Having company

over. f. Just sitting down to dinner. g. Having an argument. h. Talking on the telephone.

2. KEEP LOW en route to the lawn. Don't use the middle of the street or of any yards. If you are spotted, don't act it. Just casually, but without dawdling, head for cover.

3. USE THE DOMINO PRINCIPLE. Sack or subvert nearby lawns first. Then move outward to the frontiers slowly but inexorably, like a communist.

4. When you reach the lawn to be Infiltrated, SECURE AN INCON-SPICUOUS SPOT near the property line and, from there, fill out the following RECONNAISSANCE QUIZ.

Simply circle the rating number beside each of your answers. Then, at the end of the quiz, add the numbers together to determine your m.o.; i.e., how you should handle the lawn.

LAWN RECONNAISSANCE QUIZ

1. Is there a dog at home?
   (If not, proceed to the next lawn.)
2. Gender?
   a. A bitch . . . (If you are a guy, fixed or intact, score: 5) (If you are a bitch, spayed or intact, score: minus –5)
   b. A guy . . . (Guys, score: –5) (Bitches, score: 5)
3. Is there a chance for some sex?
   a. Absolutely none . . . –10
   b. Maybe, maybe not—closer investigation required . . . 0
   c. The bitch is in heat . . . (Guys: 10) (Bitches: –10)
   d. The guy has not had satisfaction since last spring, or ever (Guys: –10) (Bitches: 10)
4. Breed?
   a. Yours . . . 1
   b. Not yours . . .
   He/she is mixed, you are pure . . . 2
   He/she is pure, you are mixed . . . –2
   He/she is pure, you are pure . . . 1
5. How does he/she feel about having his/her lawn pissed on by a stranger, generally?
   a. Welcomes it . . . 5
   b. Depends . . . 0
   c. Strongly opposed . . . –5

---

6. (In the event of 5c) How big is he/she? In other words, is he/she capable of kicking your ass in?

   a. Very unlikely (i.e., he/she is significantly smaller than you) . . . 5

   b. Toss up (not much size difference) . . . 0

   c. Very likely (significantly bigger) . . . –5

7. Is the dog's owner at home?

   Yes

   a. They are asleep, going to the bathroom, watching TV, arguing, or otherwise unlikely to spot or do anything about an Infiltration . . . 1

   b. Somebody is at or near a window . . . –1

   c. They are on the back porch, barbecuing, having cocktails, etc. . . . –2

   d. They are playing badminton, croquet, etc. . . . –3

   e. They are gardening . . . –4

   f. They are still out cleaning up after your last visit . . . –5

   No

   g. They are across the street for a second . . . 1

   h. They are at the movies . . . 2

   i. Gone for the weekend . . . 3

   j. In Bermuda . . . 4

   k. The house is vacant, on the market . . . 5

8. Is another infiltrator present?

   a. No . . . 5

   b. Yes

      1. Willing to share . . . 3

      2. Not willing to share, and smaller than you . . . 0

      3. Not willing to share, and bigger than you . . . –5

9. Does the lawn have any noteworthy extras?

   a. Big trees . . . 1

   b. Flag pole . . . 2

   c. Fire hydrant . . . 3

   d. Lawn ornaments . . . 4

   e. Bullyable cat . . . 5

   f. More than two cars . . . 6

   g. Swimming pool

      • Goldens, labs, springers . . . 7

      • Beagles, terriers, dalmations . . . 0

      • Schnauzers, chows, Pekingese . . . –7

   h. Unattended bones, squeak toys, or leftovers . . . 8

10. Judging by the acid content of the air, the condition of the shrubs and groundcover, and whether you have to look where you step, how does the yard appear to rate as far as your competitors are concerned?

a. A prime piece of real estate . . .   10
b. Better than average . . .   5
c. A fixer-upper . . .   0
d. A waste of time . . .   –10

Now add together all your rating numbers. If your Recon Quiz score is: –30 or below: Go home or to another lawn, and don't bother coming back. –30-0: Go home or to another lawn, and maybe return another time. 0-15: Go for a preliminary beachhead—pee and run. 15-30: Give the lawn a once-over.

1. Hit the Extras without dehydrating yourself.
2. Conduct brief urinalysis at select locations to get a better idea of your competition or future lovers.
3. Eat any food or bones left out.
4. Check the garbage, but not with a fine toothed comb.
5. If accosted by the dog of the house while occupied with any of the above, lift your tail, introduce yourself, and keep your fingers crossed they reciprocate. If not, try to avoid a fight unless the humans are out.
6. This goes for sex too. Even if the guy or bitch has a strong come-on, keep your response down to foreplay in A Once Over. You don't want to be tied to a person's dog when they get home from the movies.

30 or above (i.e., the owners of the lawn are in Bermuda, somebody left behind is in heat, it's Saturday night, and you are ready to party) . . .

Shoot the moon.

1. Relieve yourself on whatever you like.
2. Set up a chemistry lab in the backyard.
3. Examine the garbage to heart's content, eating, shredding, and/or rolling in it at leisure.
4. Rearrange the flowerbed. Drink too much water. Eat grass. Throw up. Invite some friends over. Kick some ass.
5. Bark, whine, carry on. Chase your host or hostess. Reinterpret *The Last Tango in Paris* with them in the garage, under the back deck, out by the pool.
6. Generally, act out any other long suppressed fantasies.

Then Go Home.

Do so using the same Timing and Good Judgment.

When Frank wakes up on Sunday morning and sees you sleeping peacefully on the back porch right where you were before he went to bed, he will pet you and say:

"Good boy, Boomer."

You wag your tail. You have your Territory now, know how to handle people on it, and are building empires on the side.

IV

BAD HABITS

INTRODUCTION

In spite of your impatience, one thing stands between you and the next chapter, PRIVILEGES. Learning to control BAD HABITS.

Your Bad Habits fall into three categories. They will be discussed in order of increasing seriousness:

1. Annoying and Obnoxious Habits
2. Destructive Habits
3. Disgusting Habits

1. CADD Binoculars. Spots at 100 yards: You-Know-What, potential lovers (regardless of breed or species), dead things, garbage cans, cocktail parties, fleeing cats.
2. Echo Chamber. For Howling, Belching, and Loud Eating. Otherwise: dead air space.

3. CADD antennae. Can hear a potato chip drop over loud rock 'n' roll.
4. You-Know-What fumes, etc. (from Boiler Room, 14).
5. Mobile Proctology-Urinalysis Lab. With 250 million olfactory cells. Lab business card: "Have Nose Will Travel."
6. Toilet Lapper, You-Know-What Sponge, General Handy Andy.
7. Begging Fluid, Kitchen Floor Lubricant, Liquid-Plumr.
8. CADD Osterizers. For furniture, shoes, toys, and car upholstery.
9. Growler, Howler, Whiner, Barker. For keeping humans awake, away, or driving them crazy.
10. Body Builder Thighs and Biceps. For jumping on, and getting rude with people. Roughhousing indoors. Remodeling houses. Dragging owner on leash. AWOLs. Chasing cars, cats, mailmen, and shy bitches.
11. CADD Dragon Fur. Encrusted from rolling in dead things.
12. Screen Door Openers, Floor Antiquers, Garbage Forceps, Garden and Yard Excavators.
13. You-Know-What #1: Brain. Collaborates with body part 5, P.U. Lab. Attaches to body part 6, Y-K-W Sponge, in spare time. Otherwise, baptizes car tires, trees, all vertical surfaces. Otherwise, makes puppies.
14. Boiler Room. Contents: Alpo, You-Know-What, dead blue jay, bugs, shoe, Kentucky Fried Chicken bones and wrapper, and other fast-food remnants.
15. You-Know-What #2: Scuttler, Room Evacuator.
16. Tabletop Whip. Clears low tables of lamps, glasswear, candy dishes. Otherwise, retracts to clear rooms, or to introduce self in mixed company.

I. Annoying and Obnoxious Habits

INTRODUCTION: WHAT MAKES SOMETHING ANNOYING OR OBNOXIOUS TO A HUMAN BEING?

The most reliable authority on a question such as this is the dictionary. Human feelings are based on the dictionary.

GLOSSARY 1
a. *Annoying:* 1. That which annoys or causes annoyance. 2. That which disturbs, irritates, or wears on the nerves, especially by repeated acts or persistent petty unpleasantness.
b. *Obnoxious:* 1. Highly disagreeable or offensive. 2. Odious.

To put it another way, Annoying and Obnoxious are steps up from Bothersome on the human piss-off ladder.

BOTHERSOME is when a fly gets on your bone.

ANNOYING is when the same fly gets on your bone—again.

OBNOXIOUS is when the fly gets on your bone a third time—but now with a group of friends half of whom dive-bomb your head while the other half, taking advantage of your distraction, suck on the gristle.

Human beings have more words for Annoying and Obnoxious than any other animal because we're smarter. The smarter you are the more pests you notice around your bone. Creatures with no other purpose in their life than *to piss you off.*

But before we list your Top Ten Annoying and Obnoxious Habits, a note: most of the time you don't bother us. In fact, in many cases, your own wife, husband, mother, or best friend has a lot more habits that piss us off than you do. Scientific tests even prove you lower our blood pressure, especially if we have a highly piss-offable Type A personality.

What follows, then, are for the most part, nit-picking lists. Still, if you learned to control the items on them, dogs and people would come that much closer to the perfect relationship.

A. THE TOP TEN ANNOYING AND OBNOXIOUS HABITS LIST

1. NOISEMAKING: BARKING, WHINING, AND HOWLING

• There are seven kinds of barking: the first five are annoying.

a. Industrial Barking
  • *Description:* Just barking to hear yourself bark, for the sake of it.
  • *Especial Culprits:* Collies, cocker spaniels, schnauzers, Lhasa Apsos.

b. Choir Barking
  • *Description:* Barking because somebody else in the neighborhood has started barking and continues to do so because they now think you started it.
  • *Culprits:* Same as above, plus Airedales, beagles, Chihuahuas, Irish setters, German shepherds.

c. Protest Barking
  • *Description:* Barking to draw attention to an unfair situation that is being inflicted on you—like being locked in the garage during a cocktail party, after an unsuccessful lawn infiltration, etc.
  • *Culprits:* Everybody.

d. Hortatory Barking
  • *Description:* Barking to induce people to serve you dinner faster; to get more generous with leftovers; to remind them you get a yummy after *every* trick *attempt*, not after ten perfect ones; to let them know you're at the door and want

back in, even though you were back in or out only two minutes ago, and not during a commercial.
- *Culprits:* Everybody.

e. Chinese-Water-Torture Barking
- *Description:* Continuing to bark after a human has specifically told you to shut up, and mentioned your life expectancy, too.
- *Culprits:* Pekingese, Shih Tzus, Lhasa Apsos.

The last two kinds of barking are OK. In fact it annoys us if you *don't* bark in these cases.

f. Business Barking
- *Description:* Barking when somebody knocks on the door, drives in the drive, especially if they're a pervert or a killer.

g. Recreational Barking
- *Description:* Barking just to let everybody know what a fantastic, spunky ass mood you are in when vacationing with Frank, Sheila, and the kids; out on the boat; playing frisbee; treeing a cat; on a running jag with your friends on Sunday afternoon in the backyard; and so on.

Notes: Now, of the first five Annoying Barks, by far the most pesky to human beings, without doubt, is: the All-Night Industrial. For two reasons: 1. It doesn't stop. 2. It has no apparent motive other than to drive us crazy. The Choir Bark falls into the same category since it usually accompanies the All-Night Industrial. Of course, as far as you dogs are concerned, these two barks are among your most indispensable means of communication that people just don't understand.

WHINING

Since whining isn't as loud as barking and you often make up for this by bending your notes, it can be no less annoying to people than an All-Night Industrial.

We can put up with whining in small doses and under two conditions. 1. If you have really hurt yourself: not just something in your paw nobody can find, or a scratch from the cat—but a real injury. Or 2. When you seriously think you might be coming down with something—a life-threatening illness.

Other than that, don't whine.

HOWLING

Many of you don't have a problem here, especially Chihuahuas, Pomeranians, toys generally. But if the spirit moves you to join in with a fire truck one night, go ahead. Your people might be amused for the first minute or two. It's a novelty. Just make sure it stays that way.

Culprits: German shepherds, huskies, Samoyeds, malamutes, all wolf relatives.

2. LOUD EATING, DRINKING, OR BELCHING

Self-explanatory.

Culprits: Labs, Saint Bernards, Newfoundlands.

3. SPRINTING AND ROUGHHOUSING INDOORS

This usually occurs, as you know, with children or other dogs in the house. The furniture serves as obstacle course and/or home base. But even if the kids have started it, don't think Frank is going to forget you when he gets home with his belt.

Culprits: All puppies at heart.

4. MUSICAL HOUSE

Procedure: ask to come in right after your people have just let you out, but as if you have already gone to the bathroom; then, a minute after getting back in, ask to go out again, urgently, as if you haven't gone to the bathroom after all.

Culprits: Poodles.

5. BEGGING AND DROOLING

Sometimes people like to see you beg; sometimes they don't. When they do, they will say, "Beg." When they don't, they will say, "NO," "DOWN!" or "BACK!"

As for drooling, people do not like to see stalactites forming at the corners of your mouth. Or to clean them off the kitchen floor. Or to skate on them

Culprits: Begging: everybody. Drooling: Saint Bernards.

6. SMELLING PEOPLE

Especially certain parts of their body. Women at certain times. At cocktail parties. When your nose is dirty, wet, or cold.

Culprits: Hounds. Sporting dogs.

7. JUMPING ON PEOPLE

Muddy paws make it even more annoying.

Culprits: Big dogs, especially guys.

8. DRAGGING PEOPLE ON A LEASH

Not all of us like to feel like a Wells Fargo man when taking you for a walk.

Culprits: Big guys, intact.

9. INNUMERABLE INSTANCES OF IRRITATING BEHAVIOR, FOR EXAMPLE:

Raiding the Garbage.

Refusing to take your prescription even when buried in a wad of cheese. Or throwing up your prescription.

10. GOING AWOL

Storytime:

THE AWOLER

After Frank got that call from Mr. Stansbury in the last chapter, he chained you to the stump of the oak where Sidney had lived, beside Bob's headstone. The next week, tiring of your barking and whining out there, he and the kids took turns walking you. But soon the kids were no longer volunteering, and their father, too, had had his fill of being dragged from tree to tree, and of standing by while you relieved yourself in front of all his new neighbors who might have respected him formerly.

One night—it is now windy and rainy, Frank has a cold, he is in his pajamas and watching the Celtics in overtime with the Lakers in the den—he hears another whine in the front hall, more urgent this time. Hurrying out, he finds you hugging the front door as if you are about to have an accident.

"OK, goddamn it, Boomer. But you come right back, you hear me?"

You wag your tail, promising.

Frank hits the floods as he opens the door, and the front lawn turns into East Berlin. Then he takes a post at the living room picture window. The screams of the Laker fans in the TV room make him pace there as he watches you proceed to your favorite elm and—after careful nose forensics on the lower bark to see if anybody has pulled an infiltration in the last fifteen minutes—begin methodically orbiting the trunk clockwise on three legs.

When you are halfway to the back side, Frank suddenly hears a shriek from the announcer—"Bird! Bird does it again! Forty feet out, hook shot!" He flings open the living room window.

"I've got my eye on you, Boomer—don't you *move.*"

Then he dashes back into the TV room . . .

When he gets back, thirty to forty seconds, no more, you are at Mr. Stansbury's house. With Mr. Stansbury's bitch, Fanny, who is now in heat.

But Frank is an optimist. Also, he doesn't want to put on his slicker and galoshes, get into the station wagon, or miss seeing Boston humiliate L.A. He charges out onto the front porch in his pajamas and robe.

"Boooomer. He-e-e-e-re, Boomer."

A second later, glaring out just beyond the floods as if he's got you directly in his sights, his tone changes—now low and businesslike:

"Boomer, I said get *in* here. On the double!"

In the Stansbury's yard you hear Frank, but ignore him. It's a game he and you play based on a quirk of yours Frank has observed: you come when you are called, but only if you think—judging by the tone of his voice—*he sees you.* So Frank has gotten into the habit—especially at night when it's raining and you have just slipped around the far side of the elm during an NBA play-off—of calling you with a voice out of the Old Testament, like God's. You have learned this is a bluff. So now, over at Stansbury's, you continue about your business with Fanny, who has come out to greet you, tail high.

This does more than annoy Frank. It burns him alive. Not just one Bad Habit is involved here. Also, it is one thing to be ignored by a person; it is another to be ignored by a dog.

"I said, get your ass *IN* here, Boomer!"

Momentarily, Frank is tearing apart the hall closet for his slicker, galoshes, and the station wagon keys, an activity which brings Sheila out of the bedroom. She insists on calling you herself, maintaining her husband's tone scares you. Frank laughs savagely at the idea but lets her go ahead because it never works and invariably gives him an opportunity to tongue-lash her when she gets back from the porch, empty-handed—without you.

As he goes for the door, she grabs him. "Don't hurt him, Frank!"

"Hurt him?" replies Frank. "Don't worry. I'm going to kill him."

Knowing how much her husband loves you and couldn't stand it if anything were to happen to you, Sheila now fruitlessly tries to convince him not to kill you when he finds you.

A minute later he is in the station wagon driving slowly around the block, window open, calling to you as he passes the dark, rainy yards of your many new friends, including the Stansbury's Fanny.

"Boomer. He-e-e-e-re, Boomer."

Not wanting to sound like a homicidal maniac to his neighbors, Frank no longer employs his God, I-See-You voice now. He has switched to his pleasanter Your-Ass-Is-Grass-When-I-Get-You-Home singsong.

Of course, Frank isn't a fool. He doesn't expect you to come when you hear the call (though the steady rise of his piss-off barometer fails to reflect this). That's not the point of the station wagon ride. The point is to catch you trying to take cover; to flush you from it; or, a dream come true, to spot you in the rearview attempting to double back and get to the house before him. So that when he arrives you are on the front porch, tail wagging, ears down, like a huge misunderstanding is in progress.

After two trips around the block and the Celtics' game is over, this, by coincidence, is exactly where he finds you. With one unexpected extra prop. Sheila and the kids standing staunchly at your side.

You watch Frank get out of the station wagon and walk toward you like a perfectly ordinary human being in full command of his emotions. Like Frankenstein.

"Don't hit him, Frank," begs Sheila. "He came back as soon as you left."

At times like these you almost love her more than him.

Casually Frank snaps the leash onto your choke. Then he deadpans Sheila.

"Excuse us for a moment. Boomer and I are going to have a chat. In the garage."

You glance at Frank, Jr., sockets out. Inferring from this that his father intends to beat your ass in, the boy immediately bursts into tears. You love Frank, Jr., too. Always have.

All at once Sheila lunges for the lead. "For God's sake, Frank, he's just a dog!"

Slowly looking toward the sky, her husband grips his face incredulously.

A second later he drags you into the backyard. Lashes you to Sidney's stump. Then, holding you by the skin of the neck, places his teeth very close to your ear.

"You are never getting off this chain for the rest of your life, Boomer. Do you understand me, sonuvabitch? *Never.* That was your last chance. You will eat on this chain, sleep on this chain, throw the I Ching on this chain. The day your ass gets off this chain is the day hell freezes over or you croak—whichever comes later. Do you *read* me?"

Then Frank goes to bed.

When he wakes up at two A.M., his wife is staring at him.

"Please, Frank. It's so *pathetic.*"

The whining in the backyard sounds like a Heifetz solo.

At 2:08 you are admitted to the utility room.

A week later you are being walked regularly by Frank and the kids. You don't so much as glance toward Fanny's yard.

A week after that—a cold, rainy night, but clear in New York for the Yankees-Red Sox opener—Frank suddenly drops his galoshes, slicker, and your leash at the front door.

"OK, goddamn it, Boomer. But you come right back, you hear me?"

You wag your tail, promising.

B. THE TWO ANNOYING GRAPHS

As you dogs see from our story, Annoyingness has two important ingredients. 1. How a human is feeling when you do something Annoying. 2. What the person happens to be doing at the time, which the Annoying thing interrupts or distracts.

When Boomer went AWOL, Frank wasn't feeling well and it was a rainy night. He was watching the Lakers-Celtics game. Had he been feeling OK—on a sunny Saturday afternoon, while mowing the lawn—it would have been an entirely different situation. Not that he wouldn't have been Annoyed, he would. But much *less* Annoyed.

From this we get the two Annoying Graphs. Consult them before you do something not just annoying, but Destructive, Disgusting, any Bad Habit at all. The unit of measurement used on the graphs is the Annoyability Quotient, 0–5. Each is a point on the human piss-off scale which, if it is reached, may be expressed by a certain punishment the object of which is: you.

0. Composed............ Nothing.
1. Annoyed .... Verbal rebuff.
2. Perturbed .... Loss of Privileges. No dinner.
3. Moderately Pissed ..... Chain time.
4. Extremely Pissed ...... A kick, a punch, a rough-up.
5. Bananas .... Your ass gets kicked in, preceded or succeeded by any or all of the above.

The variable of Annoying Graph 1 is: the major thing at the moment which is making the human feel the way he/she feels. Of the thousands of conditions, the graph only shows the ten most basic, good to bad, and the Annoyability ceiling of each, given the right stimulus from you.

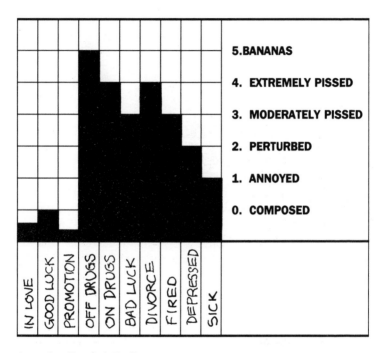

Annoying Graph 1: Feelings

Of course, there are many complications. A person can be Fired and consider this Good Luck. Or be Promoted, yet Depressed and On Drugs. Or Divorced, In Love with someone else, Off Drugs, and Sick. Also, varying degrees of possible Annoyance can exist within each category. With Drugs, there is a big difference between being on or trying to get off sweets versus cocaine or gin. When a person is Sick, they may not even have the energy to get Annoyed if they have the grippe or mononucleosis, as opposed to something like PMS, scabies, or schizophrenia.

The variable of Annoying Graph 2 is: the activities during which human beings do not like to be interrupted or disturbed by dogs. Again, of the countless examples, we have room only for the broadest categories which apply to the majority of our species.

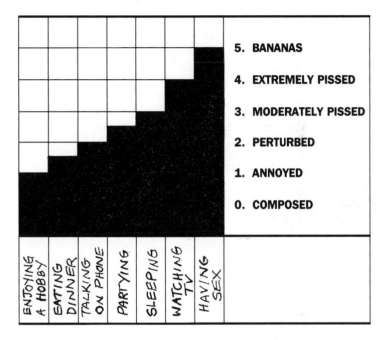

5. BANANAS

4. EXTREMELY PISSED

3. MODERATELY PISSED

2. PERTURBED

1. ANNOYED

0. COMPOSED

ENJOYING A HOBBY | EATING DINNER | TALKING ON PHONE | PARTYING | SLEEPING | WATCHING TV | HAVING SEX

Annoying Graph 2: Activities

Now, using the Annoying Graphs in your daily life is a simple matter.

Predicament: Say, one night you are out on your chain and suddenly experience an irrepressible urge to do some serious Industrial Barking. How much is this likely to Annoy your owner, and what are you likely to pay for it? Check the appropriate A.G. columns and add the quotients.

Scenario 1: Feelings-wise, Frank has just won the state lottery (score 0); also, he got a promotion at the office today (0). Activities: he is in the den reading *Money* magazine (1).

Annoyability Index: a mere 1. Go ahead, then. Bark for a while. Even if he hears it, he probably won't do anything.

Scenario 2: Feelings: Frank has scabies (1); he was rear-ended by an uninsured teenager on the way back from the dermatologist (3); he and Sheila are discussing separation because of the way he treats you (4); and, at her request, he has not had a drink recently (5). Activities: he has taken a Percodan (4); and he is trying to get some sleep (3).

Annoyability Index: 20. Don't bark.

C. EPILOGUE: THE SEVEN THINGS YOU CAN'T HELP THAT GET ON OUR NERVES ANYWAY— A TROUBLESHOOTER

PROBLEM	CAUSE	SOLUTION
1. Shedding	Summer	Do it outside.
2. Your Breath	Not brushing regularly	Stop eating You-Know-What and/or licking your You-Know-What (see "Disgusting Habits"). Or breathe through your nose.
3. Snoring	Posture	Stop sleeping on your back.
4. Loud Nightmares	TV	Stop watching Rin Tin Tin reruns.
5. Throwing Up	Eating You-Know-What, followed by grass	Stop eating You-Know-What, followed by grass.
6. Gas	Mexican food	Anticipate, then leave the county. Or at least the room.
7. Scratching & Gnawing Yourself	Fleas, ticks, psoriasis, hot spots	Hartz 2-in-1 collar. Radio beam collar. Sheep dip. Cortisone. Head and Shoulders.

II. Destructive Habits

INTRODUCTION: WHAT DO HUMANS CONSIDER DESTRUCTIVE?

GLOSSARY 2

Destructive: 1. Causing destruction: RUINOUS. 2. Designed or tending to ruin the structure, organic existence, or condition of: to spoil, dirty, or demolish so that repair or restoration is impossible, economically unfeasible, or otherwise a waste of time. 3. Causing a human being—especially the owner (for example, Frank, or whoever) of said TRASHED item or items—to experience regret, distress, or blind rage.

A. THE TOP FOUR LIST

1. CHEWING: THREE CAUSES AND CURES
• Chewing Cause a.
YOU ARE A PUPPY, YOUR SECOND TEETH ARE COMING IN, THEY DON'T HURT AS BAD WHEN YOU CHEW.

• Chewing Cure a.
Puppies, first learn the difference between Chewing and Chewing *Up*: just shredding something a little, versus annihilation. Second, the difference between a valuable item, versus a piece of junk.

Granted, it is much more satisfying to chew something valuable. Start off with something valuable, then, if you must; but before the Chew *UP* stage, break off and find a piece of junk.

Otherwise, just try to hang on till your second teeth are in.

• Chewing Cause b.
YOU ARE FULL GROWN NOW, NO DENTAL PROBLEMS, BUT BORED.

• Chewing Cure b.
Mental discipline. Cultivate inner resources and activities. For instance, on eternally long afternoons: plan future Lawn Infiltra-

tions; compile a list of everybody you would like to mate with next spring, then devise step-by-step strategies of how you will pull this off in each case (see chapter VII, too); etc. If this doesn't work, consider how, if you are still thinking of turning the kitchen linoleum into confetti instead, Frank will be thinking of turning your ass into grass when he gets home.

• Chewing Cause c.
YOU ARE IRRITATED, INDIGNANT, OR NERVOUS.
Sheila has taken you shopping again. She has left you in the parking lot, in the Toyota, without cracking the windows. Hot and IRRITATED, you are staring at her best pair of Gucci's, which she has just picked up from the shoe repair.

It is a beautiful Saturday and the family has gone off boating, without you. Frank knows how much you love the boat, but at breakfast said: "The sonuvabitch is such a pain in the ass on the water." Presently, these words going through your mind over and over while you imagine everybody on the boat having fun without you, you find yourself locked on the porch staring INDIGNANTLY at the new overstuffed recliner, which Frank loves to fling himself into after a tough day on the water.

Last week, without warning, the family loaded the station wagon up with suitcases, dropped you off at the vet's, and vanished. You are now in a 4' × 10' chain-link run surrounded by other dogs in the same boat. None of you knows whether your people are just on vacation, moving out of state, have ditched you permanently and you will never see them again, or if they have enrolled you as a participant in a new cancer, AIDS, or muscular dystrophy experiment. Anyway, you are NERVOUS and ready to chew tall buildings.

• Chewing Cure c.
Again, mental discipline.

2. DIGGING

There is not a dog among you who does not have a passion—realized or not—for archeology. Only, the problem here, again, is the difference of perspective on the subject: canine versus human. You think of digging as just relocating some dirt to get a specific item or just for fun. People, on the other hand, in either case, think of it as totaling the lawn. Wanton destruction. If, like us, you were to go to Egypt, where nobody tries to keep grass, it would be different. They even have vacation digs over there you can join now. Or, if on one of your yard or flowerbed excavations you unearthed a King Tut relic, our feeling would be different, too. But what do you in fact come up with, advertising the find with every kind of pomp, parading, wags of the tail, little triumphant chortling barks, and obstreperies? A dead mole, a lost toy, an old pork bone, a rock. Not even an interesting rock.

3. CLAWING

Especially the door when you want in. Of the three main ways of asking to come in—barking, whining, or clawing the door—the latter is the least favorite among humans. Avoid it.

4. GENERAL FOR-THE-HELL-OF-IT TRASHING

Every dog in history who has practiced this habit has met with a bad end. Don't even consider it.

III. Disgusting Habits

INTRODUCTION: WHAT MAKES SOMETHING DISGUSTING TO A HUMAN BEING?

GLOSSARY 3

Disgusting: 1. Acutely repugnant, loathsome, repellent. 2. Causing (a

---

human being) to lose an interest or intention through exciting distaste; to turn away with a grimace or, in the case of a very Disgusting thing, to make to feel sick. 3. That which human beings—especially in the case of the Top Ten most Disgusting things—ask dogs to cease and desist.

A. THE TOP TEN LIST

1. DRINKING OUT OF THE TOILET
Especially after it hasn't been properly flushed and your own water bowl is fresh, full, and closer. True, you may have seen many of us take our Perrier with a twist of lemon. But it is not the same thing. Also, it is chilled.

Culprits: All of you who can reach over the seat. (Chihuahuas, Pekingese, toys—you're OK.)

2. EATING GARBAGE AND DEAD THINGS YOU FIND OUTSIDE
This is doubly Disgusting because: a. It has no nutritional value, plus all sorts of germs. b. You throw up a few minutes later anyway, usually in the house, leaving the human on floor detail with a face mask, the Hefties, and a sponge mop.

Culprits: Garbage: everybody, especially mutts. Dead things you find outside: all hounds and sporting dogs.

3. EATING YOU-KNOW-WHAT
There are only two groups here: those who indulge, and those who don't. Dabblers are rare. It's like pâté with people: some just love it, the rest don't. No matter how it is seasoned or garnished. From a Pâté de Veau et Porc Avec Foie, to a simple Pâté Maison with watercress. You-Know-What platters are also myriad and popular, but in the interest of good taste—one can only skim the highlights of a subject as Disgusting as this.

Observe three rules if indulging:

a. If your owners call you in—"Here, Boomer, com'ere, let's see what you got there, boy"—do not comply. Ditch it. If winter, give your mouth a quick rinse with snow.

b. Whether you are eating You-Know-What on a regular basis as a dietary supplement, or more occasionally as a between-meal snack, don't come in right afterward and lick or breathe directly into someone's face.

c. Since more regular brushing and flossing aren't practical, at least get into the habit of having a good drink afterward.

4. BRINGING DEAD THINGS INTO THE HOUSE

Think of it this way: if people wanted dead things in the house, we would bring them in ourselves. True, we usually have some things you can't exactly call alive in the refrigerator, and, if we hunt, maybe even on the walls. But here's the point: these have been professionally prepared by a butcher or taxidermist—not you. In short, we know and appreciate that you want to share your trophies with us, but that's OK—just keep them to yourself, outdoors.

Culprits: Setters, labs, weimaraners, pointers, spaniels, beagles, bassets.

5. ROLLING IN DEAD THINGS

When you see the body of an old blue jay or squirrel in the backyard—the scabbier and more maggoty, the better—there is nothing like a good roll in it. Afterward, you feel like a million bucks and ready to put Max Factor out of business. Rolling in a corpse is supposed to be an old hunting instinct of yours from the days before you found out how great houses, sofas, TVs, and yummies were. So, when you come home smelling like the old days, don't be surprised to find yourself temporarily out of house, sofa, TV, and yummies. And in a bath of Lysol.

• *Culprits:* Same as #4. Plus anyone who has just *had* a bath.

6. STICKING YOUR NOSE IN SOMEBODY'S BUSINESS OR BUSINESS END

Granted, there is no way of getting to know a stranger quicker. And, judging by the universal popularity of the habit with all of you, it's probably naive to expect you to stop. Please try to be more discreet.

7. SCUTTLING (YOUR YOU-KNOW-WHAT ACROSS THE CARPET)

Problem: worms. You know the feeling. Like a chimney sweep is slowly turning an ostrich feather stern to aft, twenty-four hours a day. Solution: the old tractor pull across the living room carpet. Even if it is in front of company, everyone at Frank's cocktail party for his new neighbors. Rest assured, neither Frank, Sheila, or your friends' owners will understand. They have never had worms themselves. You would like to lend them yours for just five minutes. Maybe then they'd get you some Hartz. Or at least not take away your carpet privileges.

8. GETTING RUDE (WITH OTHER DOGS)

You know what this means. Especially in the case of a relative. (For acceptable times, places, partners, and procedures, see Chapter VII.)

• *Culprits:* Everybody.

9. GETTING RUDE (WITH PEOPLE)

(Including aerobics on someone's leg, and other unmentionables.) We like affection, but not this kind.

• *Culprits:* Same as #8.

10. LICKING YOUR YOU-KNOW-WHAT (TWO AREAS)

In the name of good taste, no need to be more specific here, either. Other than to say that it is as much the licking technique you use and the indescribable suction sound resulting, as the places you are licking, that human beings cannot abide.

V
PRIVILEGES

The Five Privilege Getters

Privileges, finally!

Since they are long overdue, let's get right down to business.

What follows could be the Schedule of any of you. Look it over and see what impresses you about it—the one big thing.

7:00 a.m. ..	Get up.
7:05	Go out: relieve self, cover tree route, border control.
7:15	Greet friends. Brief morning adventure.
7:45	Back in. Mooch Frank, Jr.'s French toast and one of his Jimmy Deans. Hack around with your toys while watching *Good Morning America*.
8:00	Escort kids to bus stop. See Frank off to work.

8:15.......	Back in. Leisurely morning. Return to toys and *Good Morning America* while periodically checking windows for Lawn Infiltrators and itinerant cats.
10:30......	Nap 1, on living room couch.
12:00 p.m. .	Lunch. Yummies on carpet. Half of maid's turkey sandwich, last bite of her Tastee Cake.
12:30......	Back out. Wait for mailman, dry cleaner, milkman, Jehovah's Witnesses. Chase cars. Extended forensics on lawn. Relocate two bones out back. Exploratory archeology in rose bed.
1:30.......	Quick ride with Shiela in Toyota to A&P.
2:00.......	Back in. Catch *Guiding Light*, followed by *Days of Our Lives*, and *Dating Game*, with maid. During slow parts, Nap 2.
4:05.......	Meet kids' schoolbus. Play with kids, their friends, and yours: red rover, hide-and-seek, monkey-in-middle, keep away, etc.
5:40.......	Frank gets home! Carry Frank's newspaper into house. Listen to family discuss their day, and yours.
6:00.......	Cocktail hour during *ABC News with Peter Jennings*. Do tricks during weather report, scoring ice cube from Frank's whiskey sour, and last of Wheat Thins.
6:30.......	Your dinner! Science Diet kibble with Cadillac chicken and liver au jus.
7:00.......	Their dinner! New York strip, mashed potatoes, string beans. (Meanwhile, from under table, listen to them discuss upcoming camping trip to Yellowstone, to which you're invited.)
7:25.......	Clean up, begging, scraps, pan licking.
7:50.......	Back out, with New York bone. Eat half, bury rest. Check lawn for nighttime bone burglars, saboteurs, infiltrators, loiterers, itinerant cats. Relieve self, bark, growl. Join in brief Choir with friends.
8:30.......	Back in. Nighttime TV. Nap 3 during ads and station identification.
11:05......	Back out during *Metro News Wrap-Up*. Last border check. Last relief. Bark good night to friends.
11:40......	Back in. Hit sack. Start in kids' room, move to Frank and Sheila's. Hop onto bed after they conk out. By early A.M. army crawl up, ease Frank off his pillow, turn over on back there, enter never-never, and start blowing serious Z's.

It's been a tough day.

Now that you have examined the Daily Schedule, answer this question: Does it look like yours?

If not, this chapter is going to be very important to you. Why? *Because it will tell you how to make it your schedule.*

Why should you be interested? Because this is the schedule of a PRIVILEGED dog. A dog who enjoys The Good Life. That dog could and should be you.

The Good Life is obtained through one of two things, or a combination of both:

1. Careful strategy and hustle.
2. Blind ass luck.

We have already discussed luck in GETTING ADOPTED. The greatest people in the world might pass by the pet store window that day, ones ready to give you the living room couch and every other Privilege no matter what. Or it might be a not-so-great person who has no intention of giving you a single Privilege even if you are smart, cute, very affectionate, and ready to save his life. That's luck. Again, your paws are tied.

Nevertheless, most people, even seemingly unpromising ones, are nice underneath; so it just becomes a matter of that little extra hustle and strategy on your part to coax the niceness out of them.

There are five ways of coaxing a Privilege out of a human being. They are called Privilege Getters, and are as follows:

1. BEING OBEDIENT

Coming when you are called. Doing what you are told to do, *when* you are told to do it. Controlling Bad Habits. People also believe an obedient dog is a smart dog, so you may get double Privileges here.

Obedience Specialists: German shepherds, dachshunds, Airedales, Dobermans, Rottweilers, certain poodles.

2. BEING AFFECTIONATE AND DEVOTED

You don't need to be told that Devotion is your forte. Or that Devotion goes hand in hand with Affection. Nobody on earth is more Affectionate and loving than you. You show it even in the little things. Curling up on our underwear while we're in the shower. Mowing the lawn with us, every row, three steps behind. Moon-eyeing us from across the room at a crowded cocktail party. Or, out of the blue, coming over and laying your head or paw right in our lap. Most people love this kind of thing (except cat people, who consider it stagy and ingratiating, but what do they know?). Most people can't get enough of it, and will respond liberally with Privileges.

Affectionate and Devoted Specialists: Everybody except intact guys when a bitch is in heat.

3. BEING CUTE: LOOKS AND PERSONALITY

The first half of Cute is *Looks.* All of you are cute-looking when you are puppies, even you dachshunds, Pekingese, and stranger mutts. This is the reason people give you so much slack then, aside from the fact that you don't know which end is up: you're irresistible. The trouble is, as you get older you become less and less cute until, by the time you are full grown, you're maybe just interesting-looking. Still, just by cocking your ears, putting your head at a forty-five, and sitting up—*presto!*— you are eight weeks again but only for a second and just enough time, before the spell breaks, to score a yummy or bigger Privileges.

The second half of Cute is *Personality.* Personality is the kind of thing that if you don't already have it you can't get it, and if you try to fake it it's a dead giveaway that you never had it. Personality can't be defined, either. It is an indescribable James Dean way of insinuating yourself onto a couch which makes it impossible for a person to stop you. Or of raising a paw in such a way that it wins the last bite of someone's cheesecake even though they were ready to kill for it. It is a gleam of the eye; a swagger in the walk; a coquettish bravado with a squeak toy or an old sneaker. Or it is something you do that nobody else does, at least on your block: a cake walk on your back legs; a Sinatra impersonation; carrying around your dinner bowl at six sharp every night.

So as not to give anybody too much of an edge, God rarely gives out Looks *and* Personality. This goes for people, also. In heaven, before making us, God says:

"OK, I'm going to send you down to be born now, the bitch so-and-so's litter: Do you want to be good-looking and have no personality, or would you rather be ugly and have a lot of personality?"

Keep in mind here that Looks decline with age, while Personality escalates.

Cuteness Specialists: Looks: all show dogs. Personality: mutts.

4. DOING SOMETHING HEROIC

The house catches fire: you drag Frank, Sheila, and the kids out. A bear corners them at Yellowstone: you chase him away. A pervert, murderer, or kidnapper enters the house, duct tapes them in the basement, and just as he is about to get down to business: you fly onto his back Rin Tin Tin style from the cellar stairs.

Acts such as these will not only earn you a lifetime of sofa privileges, but national publicity.

Except, since opportunities for Heroics on this scale rarely present themselves, you must earn the sofa through more modest but no less important displays of valor. Giving us a hand getting the encyclopedia salesman back to his car. Retrieving our Frisbee when it goes into the blackberry bushes or snake-infested territory. Helping Sheila clean up the cheese soufflé which she has spilled on the kitchen floor five minutes before the dinner guests arrive.

Heroic Specialists: Everybody with courage, large and small.

5. LOOKING PATHETIC

If you are not Obedient, Affectionate or Devoted, Cute, or Heroic, the last resort for getting Privileges is to Look Pathetic. Looking Pathetic can be very effective in obtaining a Privilege because it makes your owner feel like the scum of the earth if he thinks of denying it to you.

Looking Pathetic Specialists: Blood hounds, Saint Bernards, bull dogs, cocker spaniels. Generally, anybody who has just been fixed and/or is out in the rain.

Now, dogs, imagine yourselves as paratroopers. You have just been dropped into hostile territory. A human being's yard. The kind of human being who believes your place is outside, not on the furniture. In short, you have absolutely no Privileges. Your mission: to sweep the entire Privilege continent, marching through its three great territories—from the HOUSE, to the CAR, to VACATION—conquering each in turn ruthlessly, forever, and earning the Good Life with your five fearsome weapons: Obedience, Affection and Devotion, Cuteness, Heroism, and Looking Pathetic.

I. The House

A. STEP 1, THE BEACHHEAD
HOW TO GET INTO THE HOUSE: THE UTILITY ROOM, PORCH, GARAGE, OR KITCHEN. 7 SUGGESTIONS

Getting into the house is the first and biggest step. But remember: *domino principle.* You are only taking the beach initially— the utility room, the back porch, the mud room, the kitchen at most. Even just the garage is a start. Guadalcanal wasn't won in a day.

1. GET NOTICED
If you are chained or penned, station yourself as close to the front or back door as possible. When a person passes you going in or coming out, stare at them wistfully.

2. BE IRRESISTIBLE

At the same time demonstrate—without seeming to be on the make—an example of one of your fortes (Obedience, Intelligence, Devotedness, Personality) so that it will begin to dawn on them subconsciously that you are a diamond in the rough and your potential is being squandered outdoors.

3. WORK THE WEAKEST LINK

If you live in a home with more than one human being, concentrate on the bleeder or whoever comes closest to not having a heart of complete stone. Usually this will be a woman, a kid, or someone elderly. If no one fits that description, go for influential visitors.

4. WORK WEEKENDS AND HOLIDAYS

Human beings are most susceptible to guilt on weekends and holidays, especially around Christmas, Hanukkah, or Easter. If they are inside, drinking, laughing, opening presents, make sure they see you out on the chain, in the snow, alone, staring toward the house like Omar Sharif.

5. EXPLOIT THE WEATHER

If it is raining out, make sure they know it is raining—on you. Even if it is just drizzling.

6. STAY CLEAN AND CALM

When you are outside constantly, it is easy to get dirty and hyper. But the dirtier and more hyper you get from being out, the less inclined people will be to let you in.

7. (LAST RESORT) LOOK LIKE YOU MIGHT BE COMING DOWN WITH SOMETHING SERIOUS

Make sure you don't overdo it, though. You don't want to go to the vet.

In all of the above, remember: BE PERSISTENT. Never give up.
Alright, one of the above has definitely worked. You are in the

utility room now. Just you, the washer and dryer, the hot water heater, and Frank's golf clubs. It's paradise. You will never ask for anything more.

Twenty-four hours later, however, a strange thought enters your head . . .

B. STEP 2, THE INVASION
HOW TO GET FROM THE UTILITY ROOM INTO
THE LIVING ROOM

First, DON'T LET ON that you are in any way dissatisfied with the utility room, much less that you are in fact a ruthless imperialist who intends to stop at nothing short of Frank's pillow.

CONTROL YOURSELF. As much as you may want to (through the sheer exuberance of being inside at last) explore the entire house and get rowdy—don't. It is the fastest ticket back out, permanently.

Use your five Privilege Getters as strategically as before, but now—since your people are only just in the next room and your visibility is higher—FOCUS ON AFFECTION AND PERSONALITY.

STATION YOURSELF AT THE DOOR of the utility room, porch, the border of your beachhead wherever it is, and from there catch your owner's attention in the living room, and DO SOMETHING PRICELESS OR IRRESISTIBLY CUTE:

Raise one paw.
Sit up.
Wag your tail and put your head at a forty-five while holding some of their laundry in your mouth.
Either do a dance, a quick twirl, or get down on your haunches, rump high, and go: "Woof!" (Not a loud, brassy, "Come-on-goddamn-it-give-me-a-break-I'm-your-dog!" woof. But a coquettish, little "It-gets-even-cuter-if-you-let-me-in-the-living-room" woof.)

Then, after that, you will hear either:
Thumbs up: "Oh, Frank, he's absolutely adorable. Let him in, for heaven's sake, just this once."

Thumbs down: "Forget it, Boomer, you sonuvabitch. You can stand on your head and spit wooden nickels, and you're still not getting your mangy ass on this rug."

If the remark is a Thumbs Up, *Trot into the living room as if you don't deserve it and are overwhelmed with their generosity*— even if you think it's about time and they are the biggest skinflints in the world.

Next, *give them a deluxe butter job in the personality and affection departments. Meanwhile try not to shed on the carpet, or give yourself away by staring at the furniture or toward the bedroom.*

Then, when they have had enough of you, take the hint: *return obediently to the utility room.* Avoid spooking them with curtain calls. Don't worry: you will be invited back. One living room visit becomes two; two become ten; ten become residency.

If the remark is a Thumbs Down, *don't be discouraged: just keep at it in the utility room doorway.* In the next days and weeks, think of your extra hustle there not in terms of an exercise in futility, but as an opportunity to mature your character, improve your personality, and get some new tricks under your belt. And keep in mind: never has a human being in history beaten a dog in a war of attrition—particularly where Cuteness is the cannon.

Nevertheless, if Frank still shows no signs of wearing down after a few months, and the utility room starts looking more like the Gulag than a bivouac, you have no choice but to go for the Living Room Invasion Without Permission. Two techniques.

Sneak Attack

Bitches are the specialists. Pull an S.A. when your people are in the best possible mood, i.e., at the low end of the Annoyability scale (consult Two Annoying Graphs, pp. 74 and 75, again). This is likely to be after they have had a few drinks, but not too many, and otherwise are watching TV or playing with friends. Now, taking advantage of this distraction, and using the furniture for cover, sneak into the living room a few feet and sit down. A minute or two later your owner will notice you, pause, then say one of four things:

(To themselves): "Is it my imagination, or is Trixie in the living room?"
(To the person beside them): "Did you hear me give Trixie permission to come in here?"
(To you): "Trixie, you never give up, do you, girl? . . . Jesus, what the hell. OK, you can stay."
(To you): "I'm going to assume that this is an optical illusion, Trixie—for two seconds."

Army Crawl

Specialists: guys. As you know, guys, the Army Crawl is a last resort and performed under certain unique conditions: In full view of the enemy. Under heavy fire. When Cuteness, Affection, Sneak Attack, and every other diplomatic alternatives have proved fruitless. And, above all, when the recruit—you—has decided he/she would sooner be dead then go one more minute without getting on the sofa.

No dog—guy or girl, Great Dane, wolfhound, Rhodesian, poodle, schnauzer, terrier—needs to be told how to crawl. Just remember when you first feel stomach fur hit the carpet, and your people's eyes flash across the living room onto you: either make the crawl *very cute* or *very earnest*. If you don't succeed at this, you will be told a second later,

"NO." "STOP." "BACK!"

But don't pay any attention. Because, again, your mind is made up: life is only worth living in the living room.

7 HOUSE EXTRAS

Now that you have conquered the living room, you have run of the whole house, essentially. Except the bedroom. So, it is time to settle in and colonize before your last campaign. Here are 7 Extra House Privileges you simply must get from your people before you can call yourself a bona fide Inside dog.

1. YOUR OWN BED
Whether this is a cedar chip model from L.L. Bean, something Sheila throws together on the sewing machine from old curtains and balled pantyhose, or just a blanket or carpet you have customized—it is indispensable, even if you wind up never using it, by commandeering Frank's bed.

2. A PET DOOR
Relieve yourself any time of day, never have to hold it, come and go as you please. This is a true Privilege. Just don't abuse it by giving your friends a key, or AWOLing.

3. TOYS
Is it possible to have enough toys? Certainly not. A good inside starter kit is a jingle ball, a rubber squeaker bone, and a rawhide chewer. The squeaker is used to drown out the TV or phone conversations; the ball to parade in front of company and get trapped under the couch, forcing Frank to retrieve it; and the chewer to make into pasta on the rug.

4. A PLACE UNDER THE DINING ROOM TABLE
Where there is the shortest distance between your mouth and the kids' hands—especially on liver night.

5. SECURITY SPOT
A secret subfurniture location where you can't be touched by earthquakes, or even your people when you've had an accident inside, they are trying to get you to the vet, or they're leaving for vacation.

6. SOFA
In dog heaven (discussed at length in Chapter VIII), each of you has his own sofa which you lie on Roman style while indulging in yummies and goblets of celestial milk, and occasionally jumping off to greet your deceased owner when he/she visits, and to chase spiritual cats. The comfort and well-being you will experience on

this heavenly sofa can only be compared to that of your former worldly, material sofa. For a dog, sofas are religion. There is not an atheist among you.

The great hurdle in getting an earthly sofa is convincing your people that you won't smell it up, shed on it, jump on it with dirty paws, infest it with ticks or fleas, or lick your You-Know-What on it—none of which of course is a problem in heaven.

7. EATING YUMMIES ON THE RUG

As you know, the taste of a yummy (Milk Bone, Chew Treat, Bonz) largely depends on what you have got under it: dirt, grass, cement, linoleum, parquet, or carpet. A carpet chew is far and away the best but varies tremendously according to the quality of the carpet. Eating on an in-and-out doesn't compare with a plush Oriental. For example, the yummy is usually administered in the kitchen, and while dashing it from there to the living room, you chomp on it a few times and accumulate a good deal of slobber in your mouth. Now, when you spew the yummy chunks and slobber all over, you want a good Oriental to catch it. Still, human beings refuse to see your reasoning on this, though they invariably prefer theirs hors d'oeuvres on china.

C. STEP 3, GUERRILLA WAR
HOW TO GET FROM THE LIVING ROOM TO THE BEDROOM

We can't be too long-winded here. The story of Boomer, The Thunder, and Frank's Pillow is coming up, and tells everything. Suffice it to say now that where getting into the utility room required persistence, the living room daring and personality, getting into the bedroom takes all of this plus *stealth and cunning.*

D. STEP 4, STORYTIME
BOOMER, THE THUNDER, AND FRANK'S PILLOW

It is about one A.M. now, Boomer, and you have just seen the lights go off in the bedroom after the *Tonight* Show, as usual. All at once a clap of thunder roars outside over Fanny's house, and you immediately proceed to your security spot in the hall linen closet.

Millennia ago your species discovered that thunder is a huge, invisible mouth in the sky which feeds on one earthly creature exclusively, sucking up entire populations of them—golden retrievers, boxers, Dobermans, toy poodles—through the chimneys of their houses. Furthermore, every dog knows there is only one antidote: securing yourself under the bed of the human beings you love, before the suction starts. Or, in extreme cases, getting in bed with them, on their pillow.

So, now, suddenly, you hear a far more terrible roar—"VaRooo-OOOM ha HaaAAA!" It is directly over your own chimney this time, not Fanny's. You leave the linen closet. And, a second later, find yourself in the master bedroom.

Gingerly, very gingerly, you lower your right paw onto the quilt, inches from the two teepees formed by Frank's feet.

At present Frank is snoring lightly, oblivious to the thunder. His mind is occupied instead by some surreal predream sequence involving himself, Sheila, and the kids on vacation. Or an actress Johnny Carson interviewed moments ago. In any case, nothing about the reality of being sucked through the chimney. (Human beings are remarkable this way—the sheer cockiness of their ignorance. Which is why they are the best species to be in bed with in times of danger.)

Panting audibly now, eyes incandescent, you gingerly, very gingerly, lower your other paw onto the quilt. And, by mistake, graze Frank's foot under the covers.

Suddenly his head ricochets from the pillow, bleary-eyed.

"Sheila? . . . Honey?"

For the last hour, since putting down Danielle Steel's latest novel, Sheila, eyes shut, mouth open, in a blue negligee, has been mumbling incoherent non sequiturs about her deceased grandmother.

In short, neither Frank nor Sheila has any idea that you are in the bedroom now. Or that you've visited it regularly, on a guerrilla basis, for more than a month. You have been very careful about loud breathing, nightmares, and quadracycle workouts on your back. And, during conscious periods, about licking your You-Know-What, an activity which can arouse Frank from coma.

Frank and Sheila have remained in the ozone every night except a few. Those when they have had too much to drink, and staggered into the bathroom. And once a week—Friday nights— when they have sexual intercourse. The sound of your owners having sex is very fascinating, and reminds you of you and Fanny, Mr. Stansbury's dalmatian. And the non-Friday nights have a familiar ring, too.

"Sheila? Please."

"For heaven's sake, Frank, will you stop pawing. I'm exhausted. It's Wednesday."

"Look. I've got needs."

"Don't we all, Frank."

You've heard the same retort yourself. And not just from dalmatians. It makes you sympathize with Frank in spite of the fact that his dry spells are only a week, yours are six months, and when you come back from the water fountain, he's the one who beats you up, not Sheila.

But there are rare nights—it's happened twice since your bedroom guerrilla work—when suddenly you hear your mistress's voice in the darkness, throaty and a little terrifying as if she has been possessed by Danielle Steel.

"Frank, are you still awake? Frank, darling?"

She starts with his foot.

So, just now, when you graze his foot by accident and hear, "Sheila? . . . Honey?" You freeze.

But just at that very instant, "KaBloooOOOM ha HAAA!"

Now, suddenly, everything happens very fast.

Airborne, you touch down, all fours, on the bed, right between Frank and Sheila! The Thunder roars down the chimney and through the living room! And hardly have you begun an army scramble for the pillows before two screams ring out—

"Sheila? Honey!"

"Will you stop *pawing* me, Frank? It's Wednesday!"

Just then with the last and terriblest crash of Thunder, you launch for the headboard! The lights flash on! And when you open your eyes, you find Frank and Sheila on either side of you in bed, open-mouthed—

"Boomer!"

Shaking like an engine, tongue out, you are in a fetal position on Frank's pillow. Your eyes, large as planets, are fixed on the bedroom doorway. In it stands the Thunder itself, its enormous jaws churning—

Your head recoils against Sheila. She throws her arm around you. You feel your fur next to the blue negligee.

"Good God, Frank. The poor baby is absolutely petrified."

Frank thinks he is still dreaming. "Of what?"

The Thunder rumbles and grumbles in the door.

Sheila glances back from there. "What do you think? Let him stay—please?"

Suddenly Frank collapses into the covers as if with exhaustion. "I'm losing my goddamn marbles, I swear to God. I'm *sleeping* with this sonuvabitch now." Then he thrashes a corner of his pillow free out from under you. "You mind sharing for Chrissake!"

You give him half.

After he kills the light, you gently lay your head down between his and Sheila's.

Now, falling into a deep, warm sleep, you listen to the Thunder fly out the chimney and away searching for another house where the people might not love their dog enough to give him their pillow.

And from this day on, you have bedroom privileges.

II. The Car

INTRODUCTION: "AIR IN YOUR HAIR"

For you dogs the car is the most popular invention of all time. In future years it may be replaced by the rocket ship. Only, now the average dog owner cannot afford a rocket ship. Also, in a rocket ship you can't ride with your front paws out the window. Relieving yourself on the moon, in a space suit, in weightlessness, would be a problem, too. In past years there was the buckboard. But buckboards didn't have radios, upholstery, air-conditioning, or shocks; you usually didn't get to ride in them anyway; and, besides, you could cover more ground on foot, without breakdowns. On the other hand, the car—its manufacturers having recognized and eliminated the drawbacks of every other form of transportation, past and future—is the perfect vehicle.

The car has redefined Territory and Adventure for dogs in terms of service stations, shopping plazas, rest stops, and prodigious interstates—things inconceivable to your ancestors Before Ford. Then, travel was a means. In the modern age, travel for dogs and people has become an end in itself.

True, the first few times you rode in a car you probably threw up. But that's natural. Everybody throws up in a car at first. It's called Car Sickness. You were a puppy, had just gotten Adopted, and they were driving you down to get your shots.

Suddenly, overnight, you change. The car becomes your obsession. People can tell this just by the way a Chihuahua rides on the dash or headrest of a Toyota, a Great Dane out the window of a Lincoln convertible, an Old English in the rumble seat of a Hudson—air in your hair, eyes wide with the flight of sixty-mile-per-hour neighborhoods, ears forming F-1 wings at the back of your head, like Mercury. You're riding!

There is nothing like a car.

Besides, after you have conquered the utility room, living room, bedroom, and Frank's pillow, you feel the need for fresh air, new places, and the challenge of a new campaign.

A. THE SEVEN DOG TRAFFIC LAWS

Whether you are a show poodle or a mutt, don't despair—your dream-car is waiting for you, complete with your own personal chauffeur, your owner. To get your rider's license, you have only to follow the Seven Dog Traffic Laws.

1. Be calm, keep your seat, and don't jump out the window, or try to hang more than 8.
2. Don't lie on the horn, stick shift, air-conditioning vents, or accelerator.
3. If you need to throw up, relieve yourself, or have gas—let the driver know in plenty of time.
4. Don't drink and drive (or refuse a sobriety test).
5. Avoid activities distracting to the driver: barking and whining, licking your Y-K-W, eating upholstery, etc.
6. Remain neutral in traffic emergencies: getting rear-ended; shot at or caught in freeway crossfire; chased, heckled, or barked at by other dogs.
7. Refrain from attacking human beings in uniform: highway patrolmen, toll-booth attendants, AAA tow-truck man, Hell's Angels.

B. GETTING RUN OVER

If the good thing about cars is riding, the down side is Getting Run Over. We won't go into unnecessary specifics about the sensation of Getting Run Over: what a Delta 88 grill feels like at 70 mph, or being caught in the wheel well, or on the drive shaft. The more important issue is general: nobody on earth gets run over more than you dogs.

Think about it. Is there one of you reading now who, if you haven't been run over personally, doesn't at least have friends and relatives who have been run over, some many times?

The human feeling on this subject is simple. Few of us like to run over dogs, or don't feel terrible when we do. So, we would like to see your reasons for running out in front of our cars listed in such a way as to point out their fallacy, and make you look both ways before crossing the street from now on.

Reason 1: For some reason you don't associate stepping out in front of a moving car with getting run over by it.

Reason 2: You do associate the two, but think it is nothing that can hurt too bad, much less send you to the vet's or to dog heaven.

Reason 3: You figure, as a pedestrian, you have the right of way.

Reason 4: You don't have Car Privileges, you are grounded, bored, and pissed, and feel a tremendous sense of release and vindication when beating a four-thousand pound piece of metal at chicken.

Reason 5: You do have Car Privileges, so when you are not riding you feel it is only fair that nobody else should be allowed to ride, either.

Reason 6: Getting run over impresses your friends.

In conclusion, whatever your reason for stepping in front of cars, forget it. Because the result is always the same in the long run: you just Get Run Over.

III. Epilogue: Vacation

You have now completed House Privileges, own a car, hold a valid rider's license, and when you are not riding you are not Getting Run Over. In short, you have earned the Good Life: the daily schedule at the beginning of this chapter is yours. The fight has been hard, you have fully exploited the five Privilege Getters in your arsenal, and now you need only one last thing:

A Vacation.

Yellowstone, Antigua, Paris, Coney Island—it doesn't matter.

However, there is an obstacle. Human beings don't believe dogs need vacations. That the whole notion is—except in the case of you sled and police dogs, retrievers, trackers, rounders, seeing eyes, and other professionals—ridiculous. How can anyone who sits around all day and whose life *is* a vacation, need a vacation?

Enjoying dinner in Monte Carlo, Sheila says, "I wonder how Boomer is doing in the kennel."

Without even looking up from his shrimp cocktail, Frank says, "Who gives a shit?"

It is this kind of attitude some of you are up against. Complete ignorance of the fact that Privilege getting is the most ennervating, exhausting, and unappreciated work around.

However, as a Privilege veteran now, you don't let callousness discourage you. When your people return from vacation, you simply make them feel so guilty for leaving you behind that, by next year, they won't dream of taking another without you. Or, if for some reason they try it, you simply refuse to get out of the car when you arrive at the kennel. That is, unless it has an Olympic-sized swimming pool, a Jacuzzi, a Chinese masseuse, Beethoven or Three Dog Night in the runs, serves yummies and Alpo in bed, and doesn't board cats . . . and is called Dogado Beach, Poochey Park, or Bow-wow Bermuda.

VI
FOOD AND RELIEF

I. Entrées

INTRODUCTION: GENERAL REMARKS ABOUT ENTRÉES

The earth is a planet where everybody eats. Who knows why God made it that way, but He did. It doesn't matter who you are—a paramecium, a toad, a beagle, or a person—the same rule applies: eat or get eaten. In any given instant on earth a trillion animals are eating a trillion others, or at least jockeying into position for dinner. The secret of survival is to stay in the first group, eaters, and avoid the second, eatees. The average dog enjoys 4,380 dinners before somebody enjoys him for dinner; the average human 26,280. In a street scene of a thousand people and fifty dogs, also present (but invisible) are all the things inside them which only a few days ago were alive and well in the field, ocean, or barnyard, and which they are now using for gasoline.

So, there are two kinds of food. Food that runs: cows, pigs, and chickens. And food that doesn't: fruit and vegetables. Peaches and carrots don't run because they know you can't get enough energy from them to justify a chase. A New York or Taylor ham, on the other hand, is a different story.

For you dogs and us people, meat is Sky Chief, you can't beat it for the octane. After a good prime rib we can kick back for a while and play with our ball. Meanwhile, the cows are still busy in the field eating Chinese. Only flesh eaters have had the free time to develop civilization.

One last point. For carnivores like ourselves, dogs, eating isn't, as you know, just good afterward—the survival part of it. It's particularly satisfying during: flesh just tastes great. In this respect eating is like the other survival skill: sex. God made it taste good so nobody would become extinct.

A. GRADUATING FROM SPAM

If eating is one of your biggest pleasures, dogs, why then does the food humans give you so often leave you flat? And what can you do about it?

Years ago, before you decided to move in with people, you fed yourself; say, a deer on Monday, a couple of rabbits Thursday, a caribou toward the end of the week, and leftovers in-between. Today, now that you have resigned your diet to us, you get Kibbles 'n Bits, Gravy Train, Gaines Burgers, Alpo beef chunk, Cadillac, Skippy, etc. Every day, day after day, cold. True, you didn't eat so regularly in the old days, but at least there was some variety and no soy extenders. And it was hot.

Still, having kibble in the kitchen with dinner music beats getting outrun by a caribou after a three-day stalk. You have always appreciated people's generosity. Except while you're eating your rations, you can't help smelling the chateaubriand and pota- toes with sour cream, bacon, and chives in the dining room, or even just the chicken McNuggets, Burritos Supreme, or Sara Lee cheesecake. You can't ignore conversations like:

"This is the tenderest chateau we've ever had, Frank."

"Sheila, the taste is unbelievable. And God—the juice. I feel like I'm having sex."

"Remember this is just foreplay, darling. Save room for the mousse."

Though you realize that your kibble, even the cheapest kibble, is better for you, your especial passion for our junk food remains irrepressible. Whether you are a dachshund, a Saint Bernard, or Pekingese, you have to exercise self-control beyond human imagination not to kill for a Cheeso, a Hostess cupcake, or a simple Lorna Doon. Nor can humans debate your position on cholesterol, preservatives, salt, sugar, and carcinogens:

"What the hell—I'm only living till I'm twelve anyway."

But the fact doesn't make us more generous with the Cheesos.

Ten Commandments for Diet Improvement

How then *do* you Graduate from SPAM and get your people to serve you at least Alpo, KalKan, Cadillac, or Science?

Simply follow the Ten Commandments for Diet Improvement.

Thou Shalt:

1. Be a good dog, exercising your five privilege getters: Obedience, Affection, Cuteness, Heroism, Looking Pathetic.
2. Be discriminating (but not a Fusser or Inhaler) (see pages 110–111).
3. Mind your manners.
4. Beg in good taste: with quiet persistence, without being pushy (see pages 113–114).
5. Control your drooling.

Thou Shalt Not:

6. Steal food (unless it's life or death) (see pages 114–115).
7. Neglect yummy and bone etiquette.
8. Eat inedibles (corpses, dirt, Y-K-W, Decon, Puss & Boots, soap, etc.), nonedibles (furniture, carpet, human clothing,

electric cords, soda cans, etc.) or dog psychedelics (LSD, peyote, Angel Dust, crack, Frank's gym socks, bugs, cat scat, etc.).

9. Habitually throw up (see pages 115–116).
10. Gain too much weight (see page 116).

B. THE FIVE DOG EATERS: A SHORT ENCYCLOPEDIA

There are five kinds of dog eaters: Inhalers, Sloppers, Fussers, Anorexics, and Normals. For the best diet and the least annoyance to humans, try to be the fifth.

1. INHALERS

Description:

The INHALER does not chew his food, he launches it to his stomach via a two-step suction many times stronger than an industrial Hoover.

Step #1: Kibble is airlifted out of bowl into Inhaler's mouth.

Intermission: Kibble is held there for a split second, accumulating air pressure and STP Drool.

Step #2: With second gasp, kibble flies into throat, ricocheting off the back of it into stomach where Inhaler's digestive piranha take over.

Notes:

In the ten seconds it takes the Inhaler to finish a bowl of Gravy Train, he is not to be fooled with.

The Inhaler is the only canine on earth who will eat broccoli without hollandaise. Reason: He doesn't know it's broccoli without hollandaise.

The owner of an Inhaler can often be identified by his artificial arm fitted shortly after he handed his dog a yummy, and before he knew he was an Inhaler.

Members: Working huskies, Saints, Newfoundlands, hounds, Dobermans, rotts, mastiffs, retrievers. Especially guys. Most labs and Chesapeakes, working or not. or fixed.

2. SLOPPERS

Description:

Like a front-end loader on a construction job, the Slopper takes complete mouthfuls of dinner, dropping three quarters of each until slop covers the floor around his bowl. Then, in a sequence that seems random to humans but which is very scientific, he inspects and eats the slop kibble by kibble, beef chunk by beef chunk.

Notes:

Some time later everything inside the bowl and out is miraculously gone except for one thing: the Slopper's heartworm pill, a piece of cat food, or broccoli.

Members: Shepherds, sheepdogs, collies, setters, spaniels, dalmatians. Or anyone naturally sloppy. Or afraid of being poisoned.

3. FUSSERS

Description:

You Fussers meander over to your dinner, give it a single whiff, then glance at your owner skeptically or with ill-concealed disgust. Your owner replies, "Eat it, Fifi!" At length you take a bored or begrudging bite. Then: a. You chew on it five minutes, finally spit out half, and meander away. b. You return shortly to see if it has turned into filet mignon. Instead, it is now cold, soggy, scabbed over, and a fly has claimed it. You begin to leave again. c. Suddenly your owner cries, *"Eat it!"* or "Please, sweetie—for Mommie!" and adds an old piece of toast, some Velveeta cheese, or the rest of his/her prime rib. If the latter, you break down.

Notes:

Playing the Fusser on occasion can be a good way to improve your rations. But don't push it: humans can easily be driven to an eat-it-or-starve position.

Members: Advanced Sloppers. Elitists and little pampered connoisseurs: Afghans, poodles, papillons, Pekingese, Maltese, Pomeranians, Chinese Imperial Ch'ins. Anybody getting cat food. Homesick boarded dogs. Or, after getting boarded, anyone punishing owner for same. Bitches in heat. Guys who know it.

4. ANOREXICS

Description:

In hopeless cases, you Anorexics refuse even Ritz crackers, Steak Diane, sockeye under bearnaise, and Pepperidge Farm Nassaus.

Members: Advanced Fussers. Sick or mentally disturbed King Charles spaniels, griffons, Chihuahuas, greyhounds, whippets, salukis. Anyone taking the final stand: "Give me Alpo or give me death." Anyone who has lost a dear friend, human or dog.

5. NORMALS

Description:

Without Inhaling it, Slopping it, Fussing with it, or refusing it, you Normal dogs eat in the normal way: mouth in your bowl chewing and swallowing your dinner till it is gone, followed by a thorough tongue swab-out, leaving the bowl gleaming with a light saliva shellac. Then, after a drink, you retire to the living room for your after-dinner paw lick-down, groom, and back roll on the carpet—the four-pedal bicycle, accompanied by contented groaning.

Members:

—Everybody else.

II. Between-Meal Snacks

INTRODUCTION: GENERAL REMARKS ABOUT BETWEEN-MEAL SNACKS

For you dogs, everything other than your dinner—Entrée—is a Between-Meal Snack, or BMS.

There are three kinds of Between-Meal Snacks: Leftovers, Nonleftovers, and Personal Dietary Supplements.

Personal Dietary Supplements in turn also fall into three categories: Household Products (shoes, furniture, carpeting, linoleum, clothes, toys, etc.), Natural Foods (grass, dirt, sticks, bugs, etc.), and Serendipitous Hors d'Oeuvres (You-Know-What, dead things, and garbage).

The three kinds of BMS's are scored in two ways: Luck and/or Your Own Personal Initiative.

Your Own Personal Initiative is also tri-part: Begging, Stealing, Hunting and Gathering.

A. BEGGING

If you aren't lucky enough to have people who give you treats automatically and out of the blue; if you have a moral objection to nailing an unattended picnic table, or are chicken; and if you are not a hunter and gatherer—then you only have one choice left if you want a Nonleftover BMS.

Beg.

Since just one thing is more embarrassing than begging—begging and getting turned down—here now are a few tips for greater success in the four areas of the art.

Begging Domains
Tricks:
Review Chapter II, page 31. And remember three other things: a. Fit the trick to the targeted person—different strokes for different folks. b. Don't knock yourself out for peanuts or a skinflint—move on to the next candidate. c. The four P's: Be Patient and Persistent, not Precipitous or Pushy.
Cuteness:
Review Chapter V, pages 88–89. And again: be cute, but don't appear to be conspicuously on the make.
Staring:
Say the targeted item is a Pepperidge Farm Milano, and the begee is Frank. Sit squarely in front of him, not too far and not too close, but less than easy arm's length. Now, fix a very concentrated stare first on Frank, then his Milano, then in quick alternation—Frank-Milano, Frank-Milano, Frank-Milano—until he looks up, meets your zombie eyes, and surrenders the last bite

of his Milano like a hypnotized cobra. Now dash it into the living room. Because instantly Frank will snap out of it in the kitchen, look at his empty hand in confusion, and yell:

"Where the hell did my Milano go!"

Being in the right place at the right time:

As the saying goes, you tell a good fisherman by where he fishes, not by his tackle or technique. A dog can have all the right moves, but still strike out if he's working the wrong picnic or picnicker at the wrong instant.

B. STEALING FOOD: PRECAUTIONS

In Aristophanes' play *Wasps*, a dog was tried for stealing cheese. Since then many others have been convicted and shot. Therefore, don't even consider Stealing Food unless first:

- You have completely struck out Begging.

- You are certain that there will be no Leftovers.

- All Personal Dietary Supplements are out of reach. (If it's a toss-up between Stealing Food and eating a little You-Know-What in the yard to take the edge off, eat the Y-K-W.)

- The coast is clear to the buffet, the person's plate, the barbecue grill, and you're 99.9 percent sure you won't get spotted. Especially by a cat. As you know, cats are the biggest squealers around.

- It's a life or death situation.

If this is the case and you wind up hitting a roast, a German chocolate cake, a quiche, or whatever, remember:

- Do *not* eat it at the scene of the crime. How many dogs make this mistake! Drag it to an inconspicuous place and make quick work of it there.

- When you come back out, do so casually, making sure first that you don't have any telltale grease, icing, or whipped cream all over your muzzle or paws.

- If confronted, do *not* plead the Fifth, or consent to a polygraph or breath test. Just act like you don't know what they're yelling about. And keep your paws crossed the cat you live with doesn't try to frame you.

C. THROWING UP

For people, Throwing Up is a last resort. For you dogs it is an institution. Due to your constant food experimentation while Hunting and Gathering, you are bulimic by necessity. When an experiment doesn't work, you just say to yourself, "I think I better blow lunch," go into the yard, eat some grass, and do so. Your lunch returns in three installments and the opposite order they went down: Main Course, Hors d'oeuvre, Drool.

After Throwing Up, a human can't get away from it fast enough. You dogs, however—if your owner isn't chasing you around the yard with a rake—give it a whiff and maybe even a sample. As all animals know, lunch is often better the second time around. Besides, it's yours: you have first dibs. Nothing annoys like getting dragged into the house, then from the window seeing one of your friends cash in.

But here again you must concede to us. If you don't eat the Inedible, the Nonedible, or the Psychedelic, you won't Throw Up so much. And on the rare occasions you still Throw Up, leave it alone afterward, for heaven's sake. You'll pay for it in Privileges and treats if you don't.

D. EPĺLOGUE: GAINING WEIGHT

In all this, try not to gain too much weight. Especially those of you who are elderly, fixed, live in the city, don't get much exercise, and put it on just looking at a candy bar—pugs, bulldogs, bassets, beagles, and retired retrievers. Nothing is worse than a diet. Even people agree with that.

III. Relief

INTRODUCTION: GOING TO THE BATHROOM—THE GREAT LEVELER

Whether you have eaten an Entrée, a Between-Meal Snack, a Leftover, a Nonleftover, or a Personal Dietary Supplement—a law applies to it about twenty-four hours later which we all know. Pertaining to dogs, humans, and everybody else on earth equally, the law is universal. Its name: The Great Leveler.

However, throughout history, certain individuals have tried to give others the impression that they stood above the law. Indeed (entering the facilities in a somnambulist state), some have even convinced themselves they don't go to the bathroom. But all of them came to terrible ends. Their inferiors inevitably sabotaged them outside the john one day. "Back, you dogs! I was just washing my hands!" But their protests were to no avail. Such has been the fate of many kings, queens, and other august personages.

This, of course, was a divine plan. After God finished making men and dogs, He called down to us from the sky:

"Do you want to eat?"

You dogs barked, "Yes!"

And we humans cried, "Please!"

"OK," God replied, "then you will have to go to the bathroom, too."

And you dogs barked, "Fine!"

But we people cried, "Why?!"

And God said, "Because your big problem is Pride. You'll get stuck up otherwise. It's the Great Leveler."

Since then you dogs have been pedestaling your work out in the yard for everyone to see, and afterward often hear a shout from the cloud cover:

"That was a beauty, Boomer! Keep up the good work!"

Whereas we humans have installed double locks on the bathroom, steal in and out like cat burglars, but always detect a whisper right outside afterward:

"That was disgusting, Frank. How can you even live with yourself, you dog. Use some Lysol, for heaven's sake."

So, we all do it. But there are two different views on the activity. The disagreement wouldn't present any problems except for one thing. Since we're the ones walking you after meals, we expect some concessions. . . .

A. HOLDING IT

The main difference between a civilized creature and an uncivilized one is that the civilized creature knows when to Hold It. With an uncivilized creature—a cow, a trout, a bird—the instant it occurs to them they have to go to the bathroom is the same instant they in fact go to the bathroom. This is because they have never been housebroken—civilized. Separating that instant (sometimes for hours) and making it into two events—urge and Relief—is where intelligence and willpower come in. If you say to a cow, "Hold it," they reply, "Hold what?" Whereas, even as puppies and babies, you dogs and we people at least asked the smarter question: "Why should I?" And soon learned the answer. Because—unless there are extenuating circumstances, i.e., we are under the influence of the grippe, off clams, a power burrito, a bad shoe, etc.—we get spanked if we don't.

As we know, spanking a cow at any age—or almost anybody besides a person or a dog—is a waste of time.

When to Hold It

- In the house, always.

- During the Superbowl, the Oscars, *The Cosby Show*, or other uninterruptible events.

- When people are preoccupied with hobbies, sex, or going to the bathroom themselves.

- During bad weather: blizzards, hurricanes, etc.

- 11 P.M. to 7 A.M.

- City dogs: Any time in the lobby of your apartment building. Or when a policeman is watching, and you know your owner forgot the Baggies again.

- Suburban dogs: Any time during a cocktail party or barbecue on the lawn.

- Country dogs: Any time in the strawberries.

- All dogs: Any time in the waiting room at the vet's.

B. THE TEN GOING-TO-THE-BATHROOM COMMANDMENTS

As you know, dogs, going to the bathroom is a very serious three-part ritual performed with religious concentration. First, you check out where everybody else has had Relief since you last did, and do some individual studies. Then, heating up, you pinball from tree to tree, smell to smell, mystically honing in on your own sacred spot in the cosmos that day. Finally you commence Serious Business Twirls, SBT's, and an instant later—Nirvana.

Unfortunately, most people have no respect for your religion. Especially when they are on the other end of the leash. Until they do, you must accept our Ten Commandments.

1. Make it quick.
2. Make it inconspicuous.
3. #1: Guys—every *other* tree, please. Bitches—in the crab grass.
4. #2. *One* spot.
5. Keep your nose out of other's business.
6. Hold it in front of banks, art galleries, public monuments, or if your owner runs into somebody he/she respects.
7. Do not drag walker through You-Know-What-infested areas.
8. Control prebusiness twirling (especially that which trips walker, or lashes him/her to a tree).
9. Do not pedestal your work.
10. No post-business grass clawing or dirt throwing, or other displays of bathroom machismo.

VII
MATING

INTRODUCTION

The Human/Dog Sex Questionnaire

Like eating and going to the bathroom, everybody on earth Mates, or represses the desire to Mate. It's how most of us got here in the first place. Our father and mother went after each other one night, our mom blew up, and soon we jumped out.

Even so, species' views about Mating differ widely and vehemently. The following recent, nationally circulated questionnaire illustrates how profound these differences are between dogs and humans, differences resulting in serious domestic conflicts between us, the very ones we will try to relieve in this chapter.

HUMAN/DOG SEX QUESTIONNAIRE

1. Have you ever gone, or would you ever consider going, all the way on the first date?
   Yes . . . Humans 5% – Dogs 100%
   No . . . 45% – 0%
   None of your business . . . 50% – 0%
2. After mating do you:
   Quickly get dressed, or hurry to the bathroom? . . .
      Humans 40% – Dogs 1%
   Lounge in bed with a cigarette, or fall asleep? . . . 55% – 4%
   Take a breather, then reengage your partner? . . . 5% – 95%
3. Under what conditions would you have sexual intercourse in public—at a cocktail party, in a mall, or on stage?
   Not for $1,000,000 . . . Humans 24% – Dogs 0%
   $2,000,000, in a mask . . . 75% – 1%
   Any time, no charge . . . 1% – 99%
4. Under what conditions would you have sex with a close relative?
   Not for $1,000,000 . . . Humans 24% – Dogs 0%
   $2,000,000, in advance, on a desert island, in a mask . . . 75% – 1%
   Any time, no charge . . . 1% – 99%

5. Guys, what is the biggest turn on for you?

   Intelligence, respect for my ambitions, a cute smile, and a pedigree . . . Humans 5% – Dogs 0%

   T & A . . . 50% – 2%

   Bitches aerobicizing in spandex . . . 43% – 3%

   HEAT . . . 2% – 95%

6. Girls, what is the biggest turn-on for you?

   A guy who knows where he's going, has a good sense of humor, respects me for who I am, has than one thing on his mind, is tender, and has a Mercedes or a nice truck . . . Humans 50% – Dogs 5%

   Muscles . . . 25% – 10%

   Two guys fighting over me . . . 20% – 60%

   B.O. . . . 5% – 25%

7. Put yourself in this hypothetical situation. Guys, you are a chained Chihuahua. Girls, you are a Great Dane in heat, locked in the garage next door. Neither of you has had sex in years, and you are deeply in love. But your family and friends don't approve. Will you:

   Break it off . . . Humans 50% – Dogs 0%

   Break the chain, chew through the garage door, and have one passionate night . . . 25% – 90%

   Run away together, eluding Animal Control . . . 25% – 10%

8. How do you feel about the following: a. Premarital sex. b. Frenching a poodle. c. Drooling on your date's coat? d. Slapping the make on a complete stranger in the street? e. Checking into a motel with a three-year-old, your mother, another breed, or your best friend's spouse. f. Perfecting your technique on your best buddy or girlfriend, consenting or not.

    Disapprove . . . 99% – Dogs 0%

    Approve . . . 1% – 100%

9. Do you think of the possibility of getting fixed:

    Never . . . Humans 65% – Dogs 0%

    Now and then . . . 25% – 8%

    Constantly . . . 10% – 92%

The last and greatest difference of opinion between you dogs and we people involves the use of prophylactics. Everybody on earth mates without protection except humans. We are the only species to have figured out how to get the banana split without paying for it. Necessity is the mother of invention. You dogs have never seen the necessity. Every hour in the U.S. 1,500 of you are born, versus 415 of us. "Puppies? What puppies?" you guys say. "That's the bitch's department." To which you bitches reply, "For six weeks maybe, but then people Adopt them. Responsibility? What responsibility?"

Every spring humans and canines wage open sex war. We lay down the law about who is allowed to mate with who, when, and under what conditions—and you break it. This has been going on for the ten thousand years we have been supervising your sex life, turning you from a group of disorganized wolves into hundreds of fine breeds. No one has enjoyed a minute of the battle.

I. ♀ ♂ Prisoners of Sex

A. SINGLES ADVERTISEMENTS

As much as species disagree about Mating, guys and girls of the same species often champion opposing viewpoints about it, too, resulting in what has been called "the battle of the sexes." Because this has always raged between you dogs and bitches, it is the first problem to illustrate before turning to the interlopers in the struggle: humans.

The difference in perspective is best expressed by your ads for each other in singles' magazines.

♀

Young, attractive, Christian Pekingese, 6", 8 lbs., black and buff, looking for candlelight and companionship with considerate, family-minded toy stud who doesn't run. No droolers. Send recent photo (no bone shots!) to Ms. Bridgette, P.O. Box 1119, N.Y., N.Y.

I am a mature two-litter collie with papers, tired of steam rollers and jitterbug johns. I prefer my breed, but any man not afraid of tenderness, country walks, commitment, puppies, and a blood panel, drop by Honey's yard at 4135 Shadygrove. Beagles, pugs, and black Labs, and other barbarians, stay home. I bite. My owner throws bottles.

♂

Check it out, bitches! Condo with Jacuzzi, unlimited yummies, and beachfront for moonlight dip after the dunk. Owners split—neighbors taking care of me. Moi? 2-year-old Weimaraner, 28", 85 lbs., bench champ and pro stud. Usually service bitches for $500, or pick of your litter—now any breed, free! No snappers, whiners, hen peckers, or bruco cases. If you're in heat drop by and see Pete. 465 Oceanview, 1B (come around back, and bark twice).

Want to see more than your backyard before you die? Experienced cocapoo tour guide looking for travel companion and love mate. No age or breed requirement—big bitches, I Helicopter; toys, I Limbo. Will break in a virgin. Am clean, won't slobber on you, or drop you off in a strange town or turn homo on you between heats. If you have dreams or your people beat you, be at dumpster behind Taco Bell, 5th and Mangrove, any time after dinner Tuesday. Ask for Zorro.

B. GUYS: HAVE GUN, WILL TRAVEL

1. THE SPELL OF THE SMELL

Guys, as you do not need to be reminded at this point, every spring a she-demon blows into your head through your nose, flings your captain off the rudder in the navigation room, grabs the walkie-talkie to the engineer, and says, "Travel, you stud!" If you have never had sex, all you may feel is a sort of demented curiosity. If, however, you are a veteran, you are a love junkie, also, and will do anything she tells you.

Why? Because you are now under the Spell of the Smell.

2. ON-THE-ROAD SURVIVAL GUIDE

Should the Spell of the Smell leave you with no choice but a home Break-Out, make it clean, fast, inconspicuous, and come back as soon as possible. Angry as your people might feel, they'll be worried sick about you. Many dangers lurk outside your yard and on the road to the girl of your dreams which can end your courting days forever if you don't watch out.

Remember the three Golden On-the-Road Rules:

1. Do not cross the street without looking both ways first (even if a bitch is running from you, or someone is beating you to her).
2. Do not accept yummies from strangers, or go into their house or car.
3. Proceed directly to bitch's yard, mate, and leave fast.

3. STEP-BY-STEP STAKE-OUT AND BREAK-IN

When you get to your love's house, don't be discouraged if her people don't appreciate your arrival, or seem to be intent on making your visit as short and unfulfilling as possible. Nice as they may be the rest of the year, owners of bitches in heat mostly come in four varieties: Screamers. Bottle and rock throwers. Shooters. And the quiet ones who just call your owner or the pound. Therefore . . .

STEP 1:
Take up position behind a bush, and from there determine all exits, escapes, exactly where the bitch is, and the people's routines. In short, perform mating recon.

STEP 2:
Piss all around the house to let the bitch know you're out there.

STEP 3:
Return to your hiding place and wait for your scent to work its magic on the bitch and bring her out like a sleepwalker. If, when she does so, she is on the verge of heat stroke or puppy hysteria—in a word, is putty in your paws—*keep your head. Do not* mate with her right out in the front yard, for God's sake. Pull her into the shrubs. This may take some doing if she is a Saint and you are a Chihuahua, but that's why God invented testosterone.

STEP 4:
If the bitch refuses to rendezvous for whatever reason—she's a virgin, ambivalent about puppies, not completely in yet, holding out for somebody with papers, or she's a schnauzer and you're a Great Dane and scaring her—then she leaves you with no other choice: wait for the humans to leave (for work, to go shopping, the movies, etc.) then go in after her—break in.

NOTE 4a:
Essentially a Break-In is the same as a Break-Out only in the opposite order and in somebody else's house, which means you should be more careful, especially if the bitch is heavily guarded. Many of you retrievers, setters, and bassets will claw your lover's

door; camp out on her front stoop; ask her people for water in the middle of the night because you have dehydrated yourself on their lawn; or let them read your phone number right off your ID tag, so that five minutes later when your owner arrives in the station wagon, you think he has ESP. Amazing lack of good judgment!

NOTE 4b:

Break-In can be different for you city studs. You station yourself outside an apartment complex and stare up, say, at the twenty-seventh floor. She's up there in 27F, you know it, you don't have to check the register. So, two choices: You can either bribe the super and ride the elevator. Or, waiting for her walker to bring her down, you can overpower the two of them in the lobby.

4. THE O.K. CORRAL

The dream of every sex freelancer is to arrive at Helen's lawn and find no competition. But not even Achilles was that lucky. If the yard seems abandoned in her first week, all you have to do is smell a tree to find out how many of the natives are keeping close tabs on the bedroom window from nearby.

In the second week everybody arrives in Troy. The O.K. Corral is in session. In attendance: you local mutts whose owners have long since given up tracking you down in April. You commuter collies, boxers, schnauzers, sheepdogs, and poodles who are picked up every afternoon by your people and return on the 6:14 every morning. You retrievers, pointers, German shorthaireds, springer spaniels, beagles, and long-distance drifter half-breeds whose snapshot, name, and "Last Seen" appears on bulletin boards in pillaged towns on your love tour. Finally, you fugitive pro studs out for some extracurricular, nonline breeding, and to give the riffraff a lesson in style, while your owners are mobilizing an AKC manhunt. Some of you drag broken chains and chewed clotheslines; some have collars with gold-plated tags, others no collars at all; some have battle scars from fences and on-the-road mishaps; others have been freshly shampooed and brushed. But underneath you are all the same: under the Spell of the Smell, in need of love, and ready for some gunplay at dusk.

Meanwhile, the bitch is watching developments from her bedroom window, listening to her Linda Ronstadt, Carly Simon, and Phoebe Snow albums.

Storytime: "Dirty Talk and Lies"

The opening day of the convention in her yard is old-home week for those of you acquainted from past stakeouts.

When first spotting each other you freeze. Fur, ears, and tails go up. You advance, circle each other carefully, growling. Then, easing a nose under each other's tail, the smaller of you is the first to break the ice.

"Didn't expect to see you here, Sting. How's it going?"

"Can't complain, Boomer. How's Frank treating you these days?"

"I sleep with him now. How about you?"

"Cleaned up my act. I'm a new dog. What's your social life recently?"

"Went out to the coast last month. Ran into this weimaraner with his own condo. Pete. He'd been advertising. Was entertaining actresses, and needed a hand with the volume. Mind blower weekend. I threw out my spine, Pete's in intensive—blacked out in the Jacuzzi with a Pekingese. What about you?"

"Same kind of shit. Orgied with a couple dachshund sisters last week—dancers. Ouch! You ever had a dachshund?"

"Many times. That's when I first got back problems."

"The Limbo wounds, the Helicopter kills. Hey, speaking of dachs, where's Tube Steak this year? Haven't seen him on the circuit."

"Went down to Florida for the winter, saddled some insurance salesman's cocker first thing—Tubey was always a fool for a cocker—guy blind-sided him behind some garbage cans, gave him the Field Goal."

"Nooo!"

"I shit you not. He's still at the vet's. I dropped by with some yummies and an arrangement—the poor fucker was still whining. He's talking retirement. I think he lost his castanets, as in uno and dos."

"Jesus . . . Hey. On the lighter side, who's the bitch here?"

"Name's Fanny. Dalmatian. She's mine."

"You holding a torch for her?"

"Get serious."

"Good. Then you won't mind telling me if you've gotten into her pants."

"Last spring. Night and day."

"Bullshit. I heard the puppies were boxers."

"I'm part boxer. Listen, why don't you go over to Zsa Zsa's?"

"Sorry, I was just there. It's like the world cup, I about blacked out on pheromones—couldn't believe how aggressive I was getting. People have the place surrounded by Pinkertons. Got some flit pro, "Gaylord," coming in by armored car, motorcycle escort. Believe me, some bitches aren't worth it. So, what's the human situation here? Old Stansbury, your friend."

"Screamer. Threw a couple bottles at me yesterday when I hit the azaleas under her window. Nothing much. Animal control's been by once. Bunch of rookies."

"Mm. Hey, ssh, don't look now, but who's that Rott over there to my left, ten o'clock, saluting all the goddamn lawn ornaments like a fool? What's he think, he's got papers or something?"

"Name's Caesar. Been mounting everybody here, including yours truly. Limbering up. Not the kind of guy you tell to get off, though, believe me—done some time in the pen."

"Nothing compared to Zulu, I'm sure. Can't believe how relieved I am not to see him here. Remember old Zulu?"

"Guy who cleaned your clock last spring over at whatchama-doodle's?"

"Sonuvabitch. I hate goddamn mastiffs. Think they run the goddamn country just because they weigh a little bit."

"Well, he didn't get into Peaches as it turned out, if it's any consolation to you. But I do have some bad news."

"What?"

"He's here."

"Now you're shitting me."

"Check the little elm over there for yourself. He dropped by

131

yesterday. Looks like he's been pumping more iron. Owners showed up, spanked him in front of everybody, then threw him into an Oldsmobile."

"I love it!"

"Life has its moments. Except he'll be back, you can bet your ass. I figure when he does, him and Caesar over here will square off and kill each other. Meanwhile, the kid will be slipping around back."

"Two kids."

"No way. I got first dibs on her, I told you that! Besides, she loves me."

"Hey. That's deep shit for a stud—before you know it she'll have you saddled with puppies and a nine to five."

"She's not that kind. Now, *leave*. That's the last time I'm asking you nicely."

"Sorry, amigo. N-O. That's the last time I'm telling you nicely.

From here, the conversation deteriorates.

Forty-eight hours later, no food, no sleep, you studs are getting testier. Your eyes are bugged with fatigue, your veins burn with testosterone, androgen, gonadotrophin, pheromones, steroids, and miscellaneous peptides. They commute from your brain to your You-Know-What like passengers in a runaway stagecoach whipped on ruthlessly by estrogen, progesterone, Poison, Tabu, Obsession, Charlie, Chanel #5, and the other merciless fragrances of your love in the house and the Spell of her Smell.

Finally, dusk—the showdown. Somebody makes an innocuous remark about somebody else's mother, their breath, breed, their owner's mother. Somebody responds: "Come over here and say that to my face, poochie." Suddenly the O.K. Corral is divided into two groups. The stupid: those who decide to save face. The smart: those who decide to save tail. You Labs, collies, Dobys, Danes, and huskies, begin pushing and shoving. You toys head for the bushes. All at once fur is flying everywhere!

When the smoke clears, a ten-year-old pug named Frenchie is tied to the bitch, behind the garage.

In conclusion, avoid the O.K. Corral. It rarely gets you the girl, and always annoys people.

C. BITCHES: ATTRACTING A QUALITY STUD AND DISCOURAGING THE RIFFRAFF

Bitches, you don't have to be told that Heat is harder on you than the studs. While the Spell of the Smell is out sending RSVP's, she is also back at home saying in your head, "Puppies, Puppies, Puppies!"

But in order to: a. have puppies at all, and, b. have nice puppies, you have to Attract a Quality Stud and Discourage the Riffraff.

Sometimes you look out the window and see a Mexican hairless, a mutt with a skin disease, a bulldog that has been run over on the way to your house, or someone who has just traveled cross-country without cleaning himself up—you put your paw to your muzzle and say, "Who would ever have puppies with that?" Since these suitors are unacceptable to your owner, too, discouraging them becomes a must, immediately, before they become hangers-on. You want to do this nicely (a part of you feels sorry for them), except almost invariably the riffraff never takes a hint. Which leaves you with no other choice. You have to go out in the yard and bite them.

Subsequently, if your people don't bring home his replacement, attracting a quality stud can be difficult. Much depends on your neighborhood, the range and knockdown power of the Spell of your Smell, and luck. Then it's a matter of patience and not throwing yourself into the arms of the first rover who says he's got his championship. The last resort is going out on the road and tracking down Mr. Right. If you do so, try not to be in heat. It's chancy enough normally. Not to mention very upsetting to your family.

II. Sexual Intercourse

INTRODUCTION

Dogs, having completed courtship, we now come to what you have all been waiting for: SEXUAL INTERCOURSE. A. The kind people watch and sponsor: Living Room Love (LRL). B. And the kind they don't: Behind the Barn Love (BBL).

A. LIVING ROOM LOVE

From the standpoint of convenience and congenial circumstances, Living Room Love is unsurpassed. Your lover simply arrives in his or her station wagon, and after introductions and a few pleasantries, a yummy and a pep talk in the living room, garage, or wherever, you have sex in front of people. Break-Outs, Break-Ins, Saddle Attack, and, later, Getting Fixed or having unwanted puppies—these are all needless cares with LRL.

For the first time, your instinct and human desire are one. The only way you can disappoint or annoy is by *not* mating. It almost seems too good to be true! Still, a few LRL problems do arise.

LIVING ROOM LOVE PROBLEMS FOR STUDS

Guys, most major LRL problems are yours because people expect you to "perform"; all the bitch has to do is stand there. Of course, she can complicate matters by refusing to stand there—fidgeting and fussing, running around the living room, sitting down, or biting your balls—but in these cases people will side with you, and you can double-team her. Here now are the ten LRL problems you must face solo:

WHINING AND DROOLING:

Serves no practical purpose. Irritates the breeder, and is a turn-off for the bitch.

EXCESSIVE TONGUE WORK:

Often practiced in conjunction with Whining and Drooling, this is the sign of a beginner, a dilettante, or somebody with cold paws. A minute or two is technique, a half hour is a stall. Avoid it if possible.

HEAD HUMPING:

An honest mistake or an act of desperation. Either way, some girls won't put up with it long. Don't find out the hard way.

CAN'T FIND IT:

Every guy's bad dream. You know it's got to be there some place, but damned if you can find it, and you're certainly not going to ask her. Meanwhile, everybody in the living room is staring at you like you're an idiot. The first time you come up dry and jump off, you do some quick recon in the guise of foreplay. The second time, you start whining and drooling. By the third time, you're so upset and disoriented you wind up at her head.

TACHYCARDIA:

Your heart turns into a racecar for whatever reason. You *still* can't find it. She's forced you to chase her around. You're elderly, a Saint Bernard, overweight, out of shape. Or maybe you're just a terrier, a Maltese, or some other very excitable guy. Anyway, you're thinking to yourself, "If these people would stop *fussing* around me, I'd be fine." In this case, here's what to do:

Disengage your love. Say to the humans, "Who's mating this bitch, you or me?" To which they will reply, "You— supposedly." Ignore the sarcasm. Say, "OK, then, just let me handle it, would you, please?" Then go into the kitchen, get yourself a drink of water, lie down, and while you are catching your breath, say to yourself, "All right, I'm through fooling around. On the count of three I'm going back in there . . . one . . . two . . . three . . ."

EXHAUSTION:
Follow above advice and this won't happen.

JET LAG (the pro stud problem):
Usually the bitch flies to you, but what if you have to fly to her? You are delayed at LAX; hit turbulence over the Rockies; get crated next to a Siamese out of O'Hare. As you arrive at your date's house, a crowd of hostile mutts surrounds your limo. You attack the glass behind your chauffeur, you would like nothing better than to kick some local ass. But it would be unprofessional, and your owner would be upset if you came back to LA dirty. Next, entering the breeding parlor, you find your date to be an irritable virgin unimpressed by your credentials, celebrity, and provocative good looks. It's not love at first sight. Also, she's on Eastern Standard Time, you're on Western. You want to return to your hotel for a yummy and a nap. But $2000 plus expenses, and pick of her litter, are riding on your professionalism. Finally, the bitch's people keep staring at you expectantly.

NO BONE:
The best thing here is not to get too concerned about it. Go out to the kitchen again, have another drink, talk to yourself, and count to ten this time.

FRENCH MOVES:
Mating is like art: Technique is no substitute for inspiration.

FINDING OUT YOU ARE GAY:
When this happens, get off the bitch as diplomatically as possible, go out to the kitchen for a third drink, check for escape routes.

B. LOVE POSITIONS

Before turning to Behind the Barn Love, we must now cover your Love Positions.

THE DOGGIE:

Hundreds of other species practice the Doggie, but it is named after you due to your unexcelled expertise. There are three kinds of Doggies: the Standard, the Limbo, and the Helicopter. The first needs no explanation.

THE LIMBO:

The Limbo is a Behind the Barn position often performed without the aid of music, when the stud is much taller than the bitch. A Saint Bernard guy with a Chihuahua gal, for example. A good Limboer must be dogged, in excellent shape, and have no lumbar problems.

THE HELICOPTER:

Another Behind the Barner, the Helicopter (better known to you toys as the "Hummingbird"), is employed by the shorter stud with the taller bitch. You dachshund guys with Afghan girls, etc. "Helicopulation" is accomplished in the following way:

First, studs, secure a superior position to your lover: a rock, a sofa, the hood of a car, whatever is on hand. From there advise her of your next step so as not to spook her with it. "Honey, I'm going to take off now. When I land, don't buckle up. And for God's sake, don't bite me." Then take off and engage the grappling hooks on the insides of her thighs as usual. If your back legs don't touch the ground, you are in Full Helicopter and must rely completely on upper body strength, antigravity, and, if necessary (but be tender), an incisor hold on her coat. Now, in a single Greg Luganis maneuver, pull up, hit home, swing your back leg up and over your lover, and complete the spin (see under 180° Wonder). Now, dangling from your equipment upside down and backward— maintain the Inverted Helicopter for fifteen minutes. Keep yourself from blacking out and her from making any sudden moves, by sweet-talking her. "You're fantastic, darling. I've never had it so good." If necessary, lie. "Our puppies will be beautiful, sweetheart. I love you. Let's get married."

THE 180° WONDER:

The three Doggies are of course prelims to the 180° Wonder—back to back, Siamese. In Living Room Love, humans will often help you beginning studs into the Wonder because, like the rest of us, you can't believe it's possible to assume the position without being double jointed, Houdini, or ripping your tackle off. That is why it is called The Wonder. Only dogs can do it.

CHAINLINK CHA-CHA:

When you run into an unjumpable fence, you have two choices: a platonic relationship, or Chainlink Cha-Cha. Mating through wire is one of the hardest but most exhilarating experiences. Determination, teamwork, caution, and scientifically precise Cha-Cha moves are required. Being in love helps, too.

C. BEHIND THE BARN LOVE

As we all know from our teenage years, parent disapproval adds a new dimension to screwing on the sly. Not that our parents don't have good reasons for trying to stop us, especially you dogs. Your flame may be another breed, a mutt, a bad influence, a relative, or all four. Again, the purpose of this book isn't to help you fox people. Particularly where dirty sex is involved. On the contrary. But in the immortal words of Catherine the Great: "When you're dealing with a donkey, there is no sense playing Quixote." In other words, if something is bigger than you, at least try to spare your people the pain of seeing you surrender to it.

1. BEST BB PLACES TO SCREW

Dogs, from the beginning of time, the biggest BBL mistake you have made consistently is doing it right out in front of people's picture window. This invariably leads to something unpleasant to both you and the human—Saddle Attack.

So, Law 1 for Best BB Place to Screw:

- Somewhere humans can't see you: PRIVACY.

Law 2:
- A place from which you can spot humans if they try to sneak up on you: A LOOKOUT.

Law 3:
- A location with an ESCAPE ROUTE in the event somebody *does* sneak up on you.

2. SEX WITH A RELATIVE

Years ago a Greek human, Oedipus, married his mother, Jocasta, by mistake. When they discovered the mixup, Jocasta committed suicide, and Oedipus blinded himself with her broach, then wandered for the rest of his life until he settled down in Colonus with his daughter. Another ancient, Abraham, the patriarch and prophet, married his sister, not by mistake. Before having a son by her at the age of ninety-nine, he made a fortune in Egypt by telling pharaoh she was just his sister. Later, Abraham's nephew, Lot, holding up in a mountain cave with his two pretty daughters after the destruction of Sodom and Gomorrah, got drunk, mated with them, and conceived two new races of men.

In the modern world people don't accept excuses for having sex with a relative anymore. You dogs completely agree. Except twice a year. You can't explain the madness that comes over you then.

Studs, your mother is fixing you biscuits in the kitchen like any other day, when she suddenly turns into Bridget Bardot, and the words are out before you can stop them, "Mom, I need you." And she, beside herself too, pants, "Oh, baby, come to me!"

Bitches, you are with your father on, say, Coney Island. "Daddy, I'm on fire." And the next instant you are in his paws, his breath in your ear, "God help us, sweetie—it's stronger than us!"

Two months later you are having your father's puppies; or your mother is giving birth to a litter of your brothers and sisters who will call you "Dad."

In the future, to save yourself and your people from this predicament, remember the seven reasons you should not have Sex With a Relative:

- You will never feel the same about each other afterward.

- Birth defects.
  Puppies with two tails, etc.

- Awkwardness at Thanksgiving and other family get-togethers.

- Guilt beyond endurance.
  Even for Labradors and pugs.

- Moral degeneration.
  Having sex with a relative crumbles the foundation of a dog's moral fiber. Because, not long afterward, you realize you have no further to sink. And so, to all future temptations say (since your guilt drives you to escapism now, too): "Why not? I'm going to hell anyway."

- Public exile
  Your relatives will disown you. Other dogs (even mutts) will snicker behind your back and break up as soon as they see you coming down the street. Your people will cancel your couch privileges. Your cuteness and finest tricks will be ignored at cocktail parties.

- Family problems
  Should you break it to your puppies? If so, how? . . . "Son, your mother is mine, too." "Sweetie, I may be your father, but I'd like you to think of me as a brother, too." Afterward, a few of your sons turn to drugs. One of your daughters elopes with a weimaraner. Another sells herself on the street for yummies.

III. Getting Fixed

A. PREVENTION (OR RETURNING HOME DISCREETLY)

Dogs, if you want to avoid Getting Fixed after Behind the Barn Love, make sure to return home discreetly.

- Before arrival lick off all telltale signs of breeding. Bitches—any drool, slobber, or golden showers on your coat, or hickies on your neck. Studs—disguise or hide any wounds from the bitch, the O.K. Corral, a Saddle Attack, or a dislocated back from the Limbo or the Helicopter.

- If you have been gone only a few hours, sneak back to the place in the yard or house your people last saw you, and immediately go to sleep there as if you never left it. Then keep your paws crossed that they buy it.

- If you have pulled an overnighter or spring vacation, on return do not stagger, slink, or crawl back to the yard.

- When your people see you and dash out, screaming, do not put your tail between your legs, wag it too much, or supply any other dead giveaway that you have a guilty conscience, i.e., that you have been breeding.

- Now, when they grab you by the collar and ask you the big question, *"Where* have you been, Boomer?"* in order of preference:

   a. LIE. By sighing, licking them, then passing out, say you were in the yard the day before yesterday when some dognappers jumped out of a Pontiac, threw you in back, and you have been living a *Lassie Come Home* nightmare ever since. (To pull this off, make sure you are a pug, poodle, terrier, sheepdog, or other born con artist; or your people are helplessly in love with you.)

   b. FIB. By raising your ruff and barking in several directions, explain that you were out after cats, bone rustlers, and enemies of the family. (Fib specialists: otterhounds, boxers, schnauzers, collies, Chihuahuas, Pekingese, Lhasa apsos, Yorkies, and dachshunds.)

   c. CONFESS. If, however, you are a basset, a cocker spaniel, or a retriever, and those eyes and tail give you away every time—then go for truth and pity. Tell them you're a slave to love, you can't help yourself—but that it will never happen again.

B. BACKING OFF A VET

As yet, we have not discussed the vet because the mere mention of his name upsets you. But at last we have come to the subject which you all know too well, and which cannot be passed over. We will, of course, try to make it as quick and as psychologically painless as possible.

The vet is the person who gives you your shots—lepto, parvo, distemper, and rabies. He checks your stool and your blood. He stares down your throat and your ears through metal tubes. He sticks a glass rod up your You-Know-Where when you're not feeling well. He pulls teeth, gives enemas, docks ears, cuts off dew claws, tails, and warts, and he pumps stomachs. He treats eye and ear infections for you cockers; psoriasis for Shar-peis; hot spots for retrievers; asthma for bulldogs, boxers, and pugs; porcupines for hounds; barking for schnauzers and collies; bad breath, bone O.D.'s, cat wounds, and getting run over for everybody.

The vet isn't your favorite person.

Late at night you often see movies about when the veterinarians almost conquered the world years ago, overrunning defenseless villages, staging goosestepping extravaganzas in occupied cities, and interrogating dogs without papers. Your people see the very same movie but, not grasping the significance somehow, drag you into the station wagon only days later. Miles before reaching the vet's office you can smell the stainless-steel table, the needle and scalpel cooker, the blood and stool samples under the hydrogen peroxide and Lysol.

When you arrive, your owner carries or choke collars you to a chair in the waiting room next to, say, a boxer who is in to have his teeth scraped, and a terrier with a tracheotomy appointment. As for you, though due for your annual checkup and booster, you also, coincidentally, returned from a three day BBL vacation just yesterday. For the next twenty minutes, while listening to the muffled howls in the exam room from the boxer, then the terrier, you become a vibrator on your person's leg or in their lap. But not once do they look up from their *People* magazine. Finally the vet, yanking off some red rubber gloves, bursts out with a big smile.

"How's my boy?!" "How's my girl?!"

Now, calm down. It's probably just a checkup. If, however, your owner, the vet, and two assistants begin to surround you—it may be more. In this case you have two choices. Back off the vet, or kiss your sex life good-bye. If you decide on the former, the chances against you are 99 to 1. Higher if you are a toy. Vets are notoriously hard to back off once they've got it in their minds to fix somebody. A growl just encourages them. Especially in a crowded waiting room. If you are a Doberman, a shepherd, or a pit bull, don't try to take their nurse hostage, either. This just complicates things.

In short, it's best not to even try backing off the vet.

Instead, think about:

C. THE CONSOLATIONS TO A LIFE WITHOUT SEX

A great number of dogs, regardless of species, have had the following experience at one time or another: Guys—waking up as if from anesthesia and seeing (literally or figuratively) our balls missing. Girls—feeling like we have been given, without our consent, a hysterectomy.

After the discovery, our first impulse is to hunt down the vet responsible. Then commit suicide in a mall. Guys, the thought of never being able to satisfy a bitch again, of being the butt of every stud joke on your block; girls, of never again electrifying a neighborhood with the Spell of your Smell, or experiencing the magic of puppies and being nursed, and yet seeing your girlfriends keep pushing strollers spring after spring—these things are more than an average dog can be expected to endure.

Still, days after being fixed, self-preservation asserts itself: instead of eating cyanide yummies, decon, or cat scat, you decide to reap satisfaction from moping around the house and making people regret ever screwing with your hormones.

But even this passes. Finally you see the silver lining to the dark cloud.

Bitches, you no longer have to put up with studs clawing your lawn, talking dirty, relieving themselves in the garden, wanting only one thing, then leaving you and your people with ten mouths to feed.

Guys, when you smell the wind from Casablanca now, you remember your Ingrid Bergmans fondly, but no longer why making a fool of yourself once held such an attraction. Instead of engaging in bull sessions with the studs about who's coming into heat, now you prefer discussing Ecclesiastes or the Bhagavad Gita with someone who is fixed. Thinking of bitches as more than just pieces of tail, you have stopped staking out ladies' rooms, and have improved your manners in every other way. When a stud staggers into your yard, starting to hit every tree, instead of dashing out, cleaning his clock, and covering his action, you just shake your head and say, "That used to be me, poor fuck."

In every loss is a gain.

And it is in this marvelous, resurrected frame of mind that all of you turn to the last and greatest domain of your life: THE SUPERNATURAL . . .

VIII

THE
SUPERNATURAL

INTRODUCTION

Five thousand years ago your ancestor, Anubis, a saluki hound, son of the Egyptian god, Osiris, helped his father weigh the souls of the dead at funerals. During the same period, the three-headed Cerberus with tail and fur of serpents, guarded the gates of hell and was eluded there only by Hercules and Aeneas when they fed him drugged honey cakes. Two millennia later the Roman historian, Pliny, said the Ethiopians had a dog for a priest king. To the north, a mastiff named Saur inherited the throne of Norway from his owner, King Eystein: he spoke two words of Norwegian, barked a third and, after bringing political and religious harmony to his country, suffered an untimely demise three years later while defending a local lamb.

Since then there have lived countless supernatural canines. Those who have prowled the steppes of Eastern Europe and Hollywood. The ghost dog of Mauthe in Sir Walter Scott's *Peveril of the Peak*, who haunted Peel Castle in the Isle of Man. Prince Rupert's dog and familiar spirit, Boy, killed by the Puritans at the battle of Marston Moor. Sherlock Holmes's nemesis, the hound of the Baskervilles. Dorothy's Toto abducted by the Wicked Witch's flying apes, and who was the first to suspect the true identity of the Wizard of Oz.

Because they have always consorted with witches, gravitated to graveyards, and dabbled in the black arts, cats have long been believed by humans to be more supernatural than you. But down through history, dogs' occult activities—less infamous because they have always been on the brighter side—have been just as extensive. You have two constellations of your own, the Lesser Dog and the Greater Dog, and in the latter is the brightest star in the sky. Can cats say as much?

Still, due to the problems of modern life and of living with human beings, many of you forget all about your supernatural side. It is, however, the very thing that can help you the most! True, people are convinced your highest spiritual goals are sex, Alpo, and the living room couch. But in this last chapter it is now time to rediscover your powers and the true depth of your dog nature so that you can call on them in times of trouble as Anubis did, and Cerberus, Saur, Toto, and all the other superdogs of history whose unshakable faith in themselves made men marvel and install them as kings.

I. Twilight Zones

A. MAGIC TIME

Dogs, as you know, the first mystery we must unlock concerns your Magic Time.

Right after God finished making the world, seeing that the two of us—humans and canines—were destined to live together as brothers, He took us aside and said:

"OK, I've got two lifespans here. One lasts around a century, if you're lucky. The other a seventh of that—the Shortie. Now, who wants what?"

We humans jumped forward immediately. "We'll take the century."

"All right," said God, "but there's a catch. Whoever takes the century gets the past and future, the crunch in between, and will be in a hurry most of the time. Whoever takes the Shortie, gets the present—Magic Time."

Whereupon you dogs cocked your heads, bewildered. " 'Magic Time'?"

"That's right," resumed the booming Voice. "I also call it 'Slo-Mo Time.' It's a lot like what I live in Myself. Every one of your minutes on earth will seem like seven: to figure out your age people will multiply by the number, but never suspect what this really means. A day will last a *week* for you, and when you die at twelve, you will have lived longer than a man of eighty-four—some of you Shih Tzus and Imperial Ch'ins an eternity."

At this, he turned to the humans and said, "Since the dogs have sacrificed the century to you, I'm going to ask you to make a small sacrifice to them."

"What?" we asked, still more than satisfied with the deal.

"After you get out of the hunting and gathering period, become insurance salesmen, and move into the suburbs with your dog, I want you to support him. His life will be short enough without frittering it away nine to five, and he will have punched your clock enough from the Pleistocene through the Renaissance. So, when you get home from a hard afternoon at the office, don't call him a 'lazy mutt,' or ask him to account for his day. If he's just slept, licked himself, and played with his ball, that's his privilege for taking the Shortie. Think of your dog as a Zen Buddhist, or a Benedictine who has taken a vow of silence. In Magic Time playing with your ball is more wonderful and important than you can imagine."

B. DO YOU THINK?

Since the beginning of time, people have been arguing about whether you dogs think. Those who say yes make a strong case based on the fact that some of you count, don't watch television, and carry the *Wall Street Journal* around the house. Those who say no cite others who eat You-Know-What, sleep in the middle of the street, and don't come when they are called.

The question of whether you think, of course, relates to whether you talk, and there is no question about this. Even human authorities such as Barbara Wodehouse agree that the average trained dog knows four hundred words—of English, French, Russian, Greek, or whatever else his people speak. In addition, as you don't need to be told, you employ Body Language, Telepathy, and the countless dialects of Bow-Wowic—Lab Latin, Pekingese, Poodlingi, Basseto-Beagelian, Dachshundite, etc.

So, yes—intelligence being the sine qua non of all great linguists—you do think. Thinking, however, as all of you will freely admit, is not always an easy proposition for a dog. Why? Our own scientists concede that your sense of smell is fifty times better than ours, your night vision three times, your hearing four. Add to this the fact that, on Magic Time, you experience everything seven times more intensely. In short, as all of you can testify, the average dog is a sensory Aswân Dam. And so finds it that much more difficult to abstract himself from his experience than us. Every day, every minute, you have sensations so powerful that, if a human were to experience one, he could only compare it to hearing Beethoven's Ninth, or *Sgt. Pepper's Lonely Hearts Club Band,* on LSD.

If Einstein had had to cope with that in 1905, would he still have come up with $E = mc^2$? Of course not. But would that have made him stupid? No. Just distracted.

C. DREAMS AND NIGHTMARES

Dogs, if you don't have a job—retrieving, field and showing, tracking, pulling a sled, police or seeing-eye work, etc.—you probably spend half to two-thirds of your life sleeping, especially if you are elderly, and a good percentage of this time dreaming and having nightmares.

Analyzing all your dreams is beyond the scope of this book, so we will just mention the three kinds.

1. NICE DREAMS

NICE DREAM a: Your people hold a birthday party or honorary all-you-can-eat smorgy for you and your friends.

NICE DREAM b: A famous purebred, actor or actress, falls in love with you, you move to the country, and raise many puppies together.

NICE DREAM c: You are a week old again, eyes still closed, and piled up with your brothers and sisters, nursing your mom loudly (enough for people to hear from the bedroom).

2. FREUDIAN DREAMS

FREUDIAN DREAM a: Studs, your father, is about to take your bone away. Your mother stands by noncommittally without any clothes on.

FREUDIAN DREAM b: Bitches, an unscalable fence stands between you and a magnificent bone which the studs parade with delight, barking and jeering at you.

FREUDIAN DREAM c: You have an accident in the house and are immediately accosted by two ghostly yous: one wears a coonskin cap and barks, "YES!"; the other a starched clerical collar without a rabies tag and, while beginning to whip you mercilessly with your own leash, barks, "NO!"

3. JUNGIAN DREAMS

JUNGIAN DREAM a: You are on a cross surrounded by veterinarians who divide your toys while laughing at the gathering clouds.

JUNGIAN DREAM b: You lie in bed, a knife in one paw, a fork in the other. You also wear a pink bonnet. Suddenly your owner's little girl walks in with a picnic basket.

JUNGIAN DREAM c: Your breath has caught fire and your owner is chasing you around the house on a white charger, dressed as Saint Anthony.

JUNGIAN DREAM d: You are standing next to the Empire State Building holding Fay Ray (disguised as a golden retriever) in one paw. With the other, you fling office furniture from the 102nd floor onto the animal-control officers below.

Your personal nightmares are too many to enumerate. So we will restrict ourselves to the five species' Regular Recurrent Realer-Than-Lifes. These are of course the ones that make you howl, whine, and do the upside-down runaway quadracycle, terrifying your people as much as you. So try to wake up as soon as they shake you, and before you both die of fright.

4. NIGHTMARES

NIGHTMARE a: Frank leads you down a dark corridor at the end of which stands the vet next to a decompression chamber. Frank hands him the lead and turns to you expressionlessly. "I'm sorry, Boomer. You've become a pain in the ass. Good-bye."

NIGHTMARE b: You are chasing the neighbor's Siamese as usual. Suddenly—a dream come true—you trap her in a warehouse. No exit. She hides behind some boxes. Licking your chops, preparing for the snack you have been waiting your whole life for, a chuckle escapes you. "Kiss it good-bye, kitty." Then you lunge behind the boxes . . . and find yourself standing in front of a nine-hundred-pound Bengal tiger wearing a wider smile than yours. "Fuck you too, Fido."

NIGHTMARE c: Your people leave you in the kennel and never come back.

NIGHTMARE d: You are sucked through the chimney of your house by thunder. Attempting to rescue you, your owner chases the wind in the station wagon. At the horizon he finds your collar and a tuft of red fur. He looks up into the sky slowly, then all at once clutches his face, "Good God, Boomer—you were RIGHT!!"

NIGHTMARE e: Your people die and no one is left to take care of you.

D. ESP: TWO LITTLE STORIES

SHOOTER "SPEEDMAN" DIRKES, an ex-racehorse trainer, was sitting in an alley in the Bowery during the Depression, reading the racing forms, when a stray appeared at his shoulder. The dog was a boxer-collie cross by the look of him, and though he clearly hadn't had a meal in some time, Shooter continued to divide his intense concentration between tomorrow's line-up and his bottle of Thunderbird. When he finished the T'bird and his head was pleasantly in orbit, he noticed that the dog was tapping the sidewalk with his left paw, then his right, in double, repeating sequences. 2-4, 3-7, 2-4, 3-7.

The next morning, Shooter—he wasn't exactly sure why—pawned his watch, and played, in the second and third races, the 4-7 Daily Double at Belmont. He won $15,567.

Returning to the Bowery early that evening, he found the dog exactly where he had left him. Sharing with him a shopping bag of imported baloney, French bread, Wise potato chips, and Wild

Turkey, he consulted with the dog on another racing roster. By the end of the night, he had his arm around him and was calling him "Jesus."

The next day Shooter won $159,000. But when he came back to pick Jesus up in a limousine, the dog was gone.

A NAVY CAPTAIN went overseas during the war. Soon his family got word that his ship had been sunk, no survivors.

Three years later the family dog, a German shepherd named Bill, began running around the house, crying and wagging, his master's slipper in his mouth. Just then the phone rang, long distance news from headquarters in the Philippines: the captain had been found in an off-shore POW camp. He was on his way home.

THE MORAL OF THE STORIES: Dogs, don't ignore your ESP. It will shock and amaze people and earn you their eternal love.

E. FIVE OTHER OCCULT POWERS

1. PSYCHIC NAVIGATION
Tales abound about how dogs find their way home from impossible distances, without any track to follow. Since you don't read maps, such feats can only be explained in one way. Brushing up on your Psychic Navigation powers becomes especially important if you are a stud, a hunter, a dissatisfied bitch, a potential dognapping victim, or fly regularly and sometimes find yourself in unscheduled baggage claim areas.

2. TELEKINESIS
Most people believe this is nonsense, too. This makes it all the better for you since your owner, unless she is Shirley MacLaine, will never suspect.

Telekinesis comes in handiest when people are eating in front of you, ignoring your begging. You merely fix your gaze on their sausage, meatloaf, prime rib, whatever, and pull it off their plate onto the floor. Then, while you're innocently cleaning up the mess for them, they have the usual conversation.

"Did you see that, Sheila? It flew right off my plate, I swear to God!"

"Don't be ridiculous, Frank. You spilled it. You're so clumsy, honestly—this is the second time it's happened today."

"Yeah, and every one of them, Boomer's been *staring* at my meat!"

"The dog is casting a spell on your dinner—is that what you're telling me, Frank?"

They both look at you out of the corner of their eye. Gulping the last of your TK score, you give them your standard moron expression and wag your tail. Suddenly Frank throws up his palms in front of Sheila.

"OK, OK, so I'm a little clumsy. Is there any more roast left, or what?"

3. ASTRAL-PROJECTION

Astral work is another favorite with you because when you indulge, it just looks to people like you're bagging Z's, further encouraging the popular misconception that you sleep a lot.

A-P is tailor-made for when your family leaves on vacations to someplace you would love to go yourself, say, the beach in Acapulco.

After the first day, kicking back in a lawn chair with a Tia Maria, Frank says: "Have fun at the beach today, kids?"

Kids: "We played with Boomer, Daddy! He stole the beach ball!"

Frank: "Sure he did." Aside to Sheila: "Get a load-a that. God, what I'd do to be five again myself."

Two weeks later, picking you up after vacation, Frank—sunglasses, bermudas, nice tan—is standing with the kennel man outside your run.

"Hope my dog didn't give you too much trouble this time."

"Trouble? He was a saint—slept like he was in a coma . . . Oh, by the way, here's your beach ball."

"Beach ball?"

"Yeah, found it in his run here after the first day. You left it with him, didn't you? . . . Mr. Johnson?"

4. SMELLING EMOTIONS

Different emotions trigger different chemical secretions in the body, each of which has a unique smell. This may seem a dubious proposition to a species with a million olfactory cells; us. But it is simply a matter of fact to a species with 250 million: you.

Fear is of course the smelliest of the emotions: at once sweet like ginger, pungent like gouda, and acrid like off kippers. All of you get it from cats and mailmen; you Dobermans, pits, and shepherds get it from just about everybody; and as soon as this fragrance hits your nose a little voice that has been in your head since the Stone Age says "Dinnertime."

Earlier, we talked a lot about gearing your actions to the mood your people are in. The best way of determining the latter is through your Psychic Smell. For instance, take the smells of the four basic human moods in the house. Gaiety—sweet lemons. Depression—old pâté. Love—milk chocolate. Irritability—burnt biscuits. Now, if you go inside on Monday and one person— say, Sheila—smells like milk chocolate, and the other person— say, Frank—like burnt biscuits, stick closer to Sheila, especially if you want anything and/or can't resist indulging in a Bad Habit. If you go inside on Tuesday and the whole house smells like sweet lemons—everybody's in a fantastic mood—great! Run, bark, hack around with your ball, or do anything else you feel like, within reason. If, however, the house smells like old pâté, head back outside till the humans improve their mood.

5. MIND CONTROL

You dogs have been Mind Controlling us for centuries, as you know. Some of you are naturally more proficient at this than others. For example, you toys—especially you poodles, cockers, Lhasas, and Pekingese.

Like anything, Mind Control takes practice and should be started with the easier things. An ideal step #1 for Mind Control involves treats. Simply stare at your owner's head for a minute, while repeating inside your own over and over: "You want to give me a yummy, Frank. I'm loving, adorable, and irresistibly cute. You're *dying* to give me a yummy, Frank. I'm loving, adorable . . ." etc. etc. Until he finally gets up and gives you a yummy as if it's his own idea and he's impressed with his own spur-of-the-moment generosity.

After you get this step down in a month or so, move on to #2. "You want to take me out and play ball." Then on to 3. "You want to let me up on the couch." 4. "You want to go next door and ask Stansbury to let me breed his bitch, Fanny." 5. "You want to take me to Acapulco next time." 6. "You want to buy me some clothes." 7. "You want to give me my own credit card."

Master the possibilities. All it takes is faith in yourself.

II. Dog Religion

INTRODUCTION

The history of Dog Religion is long and complicated. In very ancient times, preceding the birth of Dogianity, hundreds of cults flourished: Dionysiac poodles, Hedonist Labs, Stoic schnauzers, Pantheist pugs, mendicant mutts. But we haven't time to discuss paganism. The moral and ontological roots of modern monotheistic Dogianity lie in Two Histories: The First Dog Commandment, and Buddha and the Bow-Wow Under the Bo Tree.

A. TWO HISTORIES

1. THE FIRST DOG COMMANDMENT

Moses' dog was a huge Egyptian saluki hound with one white eye, and was called The Owl.

When the Owl went up with the prophet to Mt. Sinai, he stood next to his master while the latter received the Ten Commandments from God. Fire was flying everywhere, the wind was ter-

rific, and the thunder fulminated around his head, but the Owl courageously held his ground during the epiphany. After it was over, Moses, exhausted and terrified, fell fast asleep next to the tablets. His dog, on the verge of collapse, too, was about to join him when he heard a whisper from a low-flying cloud—

"Owl, do you hear Me?"

The dog quickly straightened himself on his front paws, eyes wide, ears heavenward.

"Good," said God. "Now, I want to make a covenant with you dogs, too. I'm doing it while Moses is asleep because if he or any other human heard this—well, I'm sure you understand."

The Owl nodded judiciously.

"I have one commandment for you," declared God.

The Owl glanced toward the commandments next to his master. The Almighty nodded.

"Yes, I know. But they need those extra nine. A terribly complicated species! Originally I had thousands, except I knew they would never keep track of them, and I had the time of My life cutting them down to ten. Thank your lucky stars you and your brothers and sisters are simple dogs, Owl!"

The hound nodded at the sky, his heartbeat quickening in anticipation of his mission's revelation.

"As you know," resumed God, "I love all my creatures equally. But a father can't help having a special place in his heart for one of his children who turned out particularly well. It's not just a coincidence that I made your name Mine spelled backward. I know you bite sometimes, and get carried away here and there, but you've got hearts of gold, all of you. So, the one commandment I'm about to give you is harder than any other animal will get. For a simple reason: I know only you dogs can handle it."

The Owl's voice trembled. "What is it, Sir—please."

"Devotion. I want you to be people's friend, stay by their side always, no matter what. That will be your religion."

The dog fell into a grave silence.

"OK—it's not going to be a picnic sometimes, I admitted that!" exclaimed God. "They're a moody, moody species—granted. But do you know *why* that is?"

The Owl shook his head, but had a feeling he was about to find out.

"Because they think *nobody likes them.* Consider it—all you other animals have such a grand time together: a rabbit, a deer, a chipmunk, a robin, a dog all in the same field chatting amiably until the human shows up. What happens then? Everybody runs for dear life! Many people pretend this doesn't bother them—they laugh, they strut, they beat their chest. But underneath the facade, can you imagine how depressing it is, getting run from all the time, estranged from every brother on the planet, like an ogre?

"So, what I'm asking you is this. Be the animal diplomat to people. Reach out your paw to them, move in with them, so they won't feel so alone."

The Owl pondered the onerous responsibility of taking on this commandment solo. "What about cats?" he finally asked.

"Well, I've had a chat with them about this, and they have agreed to take up some of the slack," God admitted. "Except the bottom line for a feline, as you know, is self-interest and a cushy life. The cat is your opposite—too practical to really love somebody without considering the perks. I'm not criticizing them for this, after all, I made them that way, and everybody's got to look out for #1 on earth to some extent for survival. In that regard, I know you would just as soon be on your own out in the woods like your cousins, the wolves. You hate the very thought of begging at the dinner table. But who are my greatest saints? Beggars, mendicants! And let's be frank, it's not like all of this would be self-sacrifice. Haven't I already compensated you with Magic Time, and an array of Occult Powers?"

"Yes," stammered the Owl weakly, "but . . ."

"But what? You have been living with people for years already—you need them, they need you. Shall I tell you why? Because deep in the heart of every dog is a *person*, and deep in the heart of every person is a *dog*. And shall I tell you how I know that? Because I made it that way! Don't ask Me the reason. It's too complicated. But I'll give you a clue: *balance*. Every creature needs balance."

At that the Owl bowed his head. And when he raised it again, the cloud was gone.

Just then Moses woke up with a start. "Owl, heel!"

Momentarily, the prophet was descending Mt. Sinai with the ten tablets of man's new religion on his back.

And the dog was at his master's heel with the One for his species clamped in his mouth.

2. BUDDHA AND THE BOW-WOW UNDER THE BO TREE

Seven centuries later Buddha was sitting under the Bo Tree when, hearing a dog loudly chewing a bone nearby, he glared around peevishly.

"Hey, keep it down—can't you see somebody's trying to concentrate here?"

The dog, seeming to have suddenly materialized a few feet away, but with nothing else to recommend him, distracted himself only for a second. "That makes two of us," he snapped, then returned to his bone with renewed zeal.

"Listen," said Buddha evenly, "what you're doing there happens to be a little less important than what I'm doing here."

"And what might that be?" grumbled the dog between bites.

"I'm afraid you wouldn't understand."

"Try me."

"All right. I'm seeking Enlightenment."

"Chhh," snorted the dog.

" 'Chhh'? What's that supposed to mean—'Chhh'?"

"Just what it sounds like—Chhh," declared the dog, glancing at Gautama summarily as if taking in his six years of struggle in a second of Magic Time. "No wonder you're not getting anywhere."

"Well, well, I see that you must be Enlightened yourself," observed Buddha, bristling. "In that case, perhaps you wouldn't mind passing along the secret."

"It's quite simple," replied the dog. "Think with your belly."

"Naturally. Of course. I see. And how do you know when you're thinking with your *belly*, might I ask?"

"That's simpler. You're no longer interested in having pointless discussions like these—but in sitting under a tree all day, chewing a bone, and saying just one word when people pass by."

"What?"

"Bow-wow!"

At that instant, Buddha experienced Enlightenment.

Shortly afterward, he was seen leaving the Bo Tree in the company of the dog, the duo alternately barking at each other, then howling with laughter.

B. LIFE AFTER DEATH

Your Magic Time only lasts from ten to fourteen years. Often it is made shorter still by getting run over, heartworms, or put down. So, in every moment of your brief life—whether you are just Getting Adopted, enduring Boot Camp, staking out Territory, scoring Privileges, controlling Bad Habits, Eating and Relieving yourself, or Mating—you are haunted by one question above all:

"Will I go to Heaven? What will it be like?"

1. DOG HEAVEN

Dog Heaven is the same place as human heaven. If your owner or any of your friends from the block beat you to it there, they greet you at the gates. The news of your arrival is trumpeted from very tall, shimmering crystal towers by angels with scarlet wings and moon-colored gowns.

"Boomer is coming up! The dog, Boomer!"

Or, if you are already there, and your owner is the newcomer, "Frank Johnson is coming up! The human, Frank!"

Thus, heaven is filled with the constant exultant hubbub of

residents rushing to the gates to greet their family, friends, and loved ones, human and canine. Cats and the spirits of every other species are also represented, but the population of paradise is of course predominantly people and dogs.

When you arrive, in spite of the grandeur of the spectacle—the pink and gold clouds, rainbows, windy spiritual forests, and the electrifying song of cherubim and invisible robins—you are naturally quite spooked nevertheless, and are grateful for any friendly faces. From behind the gates everybody is flinging up their arms and paws, calling to you, "It's marvelous, Boomer! Don't worry!"

In the next instant, however, head awhirl, you find yourself alone in a room of mirrors. On earth when you looked in a mirror, you always cocked your head and said to yourself, "Who the hell's that?" Now, cocking your head even farther in the heavenly mirrors, seeing that it is invisible, in addition to your tail and all the rest of you, too, you say, "Good God, have mercy on me." Then suddenly, a Voice of thunder—

"Don't worry, Boomer. Nobody's perfect."

You collapse to the floor, head down, trembling worse than you ever did under Frank's bed. In this position you now hear shuffling paperwork all around you, punctuated with "Mms" and "Hmmmms," and even several "Mm*Hmmmms*." Then the sound of weightless spectacles hitting a desk, a long grave exhale, and at last—

"You seem to have gone AWOL more than once, Boomer. You dug up the Johnsons' garden on a regular basis. You ate one of their station wagons. And . . . I don't think we have to mention the other, shall we say 'lapses of moderation and good taste,' do we?"

"No, sir."

"Good. Now, what do you have to say for yourself?"

With a deep breath, you commence the impassioned self-defense you have been preparing all your life. But stop almost as abruptly. "What can I say? I'm a dog! I have no excuses. Are you going to send me to hell?"

"Don't be ridiculous. You've made your mistakes—yes. But you loved the Johnsons with all your heart, and gave them a better life."

"Thank you. I did what I could."

"Yes, but that doesn't mean there isn't room for improvement. So, I'm sending you back for another round."

"Now?"

"No, no. Everybody gets some rest. You stay in heaven here for a while, rest, enjoy yourself. In the meantime, decide what you want to be next time—a poodle, a weimaraner, a dachshund, a mixed breed, whatever. We're going to have to fit you into a litter somewhere."

"I have to go through it all again—Getting Adopted, Boot Camp, Territory, Privileges, Bad Habits, Food and Relief, and Mating?!"

"A dog must learn to get along with human beings in every dimension. Next time I'm sure you will make an even better individual based on this go-around. Who knows, you may even become perfect."

"What happens then?"

"On return here you are given the gold star and, with it, choose to either stay and enjoy eternal bliss as a dog saint, or return to earth as a doghisattva and help others to perfection. You are about to meet both these magnificent kinds of canines in heaven now, as well as silver stars, reruns, like yourself. But you will learn from everyone, including the spirits of all the other species."

"And to think I was terrified of this moment! Frank had me convinced I was a goner, I swear—that dogs have no soul. You can't believe how depressed it got me. In fact, that's why I kept digging up the garden, and tore apart the station wagon that once."

"You'll have to forgive Frank. He's out there waiting for you."

And with that, hardly can you bat an eye before, tail and ears flying, you are bounding through the gates of heaven, Frank and other family and friends racing to meet you.

After kisses and hugs, they immediately take you on a tour of paradise. All your friends from the neighborhood introduce you to saints and doghisattvas. They are giving lectures and holding symposiums in marble courts filled with crowds of celestial canines. Your people point out the great human heroes of history. They are also in oratory, or strolling through the orange groves of heaven, contemplating alone. In the foreground, dogs bask on couches, conversing, eating immaterial bones, and sleeping peacefully. In the background, all along the infinite tiers of heaven, canines chase felines through fields of clouds, the cats slide down rainbows onto their pursuers' backs and ride them triumphantly like horses.

After years of this life—or perhaps it is only seconds, who can tell in eternity?—all at once you hear the trumpets of the angels again.

"Boomer, to the office! The dog, Boomer—the office!"

Instantly you are there, breathless.

"Is it time already?" you stammer.

"I'm afraid so, Boomer," comes the Thunder from all around you. "Have you made up your mind what you want to be?"

You look all around. You don't want to leave heaven. But for all its troubles, you begin to feel that old longing for Mother Earth. Suddenly you straighten. "Yes. I think I would like to be a poodle."

"A fine choice! You'll make a splendid one. I have just the home for you. Your mother and father are getting together in the Living Room even now, as we speak."

Your heart quickens. "What will my life with people be like this time?"

"That's completely up to you, Boomer. But after all you have learned about yourself and them, I have a feeling it will be a wonderful one. Are you ready?"

You hastily cross yourself with one paw, then clamp your eyes tight. "Yes, sir."

"Heeeeeeere you go!"

All at once you feel yourself tumbling through the sky past fireworks of galaxies, comets, and exploding stars to the tiny, spinning blue orb—your home, earth. And as your pulse races with the thought of a new life with people, you hear the Thunder echoing from the clouds behind you over and over until you touch ground—

"Farewell, Boomer. Good luck to a good dog! Good luck! Good luck!"